D0504896

ABOUT THE AUTHOR

Reggie Chamberlain-King quickly sped past youth and education into decrepit early adulthood, becoming, by cold hard luck, a writer, musician, and broadcaster. He makes frequent appearances on Radio Ulster's *The Arts Show* and was, for four years, the cultural attaché on *After Midnight* with Stuart Bailie.

He has written several plays, including *The Ballad of Lilliburlero* for BBC NI Events, and *The Down Chorus*, for Wireless Mystery Theatre. His work has been on BBC Radio 3 and BBC Radio 4 as well as having been broadcast in Germany, Canada and the United States.

He is a co-founder, actor, musician and continuity announcer with Wireless Mystery Theatre and author of the cult mystery series *The Brittaine & Molloy Inquiry Quarterly*. *Weird Dublin* is the companion to his bestselling book *Weird Belfast*.

For more on Reggie Chamberlain-King visit www.thestuffedowl.co.uk
Or follow him on Twitter @Reggie_C_King

A MISCELLANY, ALMANACK, AND COMPANION

COMPILED, ALMANACKED,
AND MISCELLANED BY

REGGIE CHAMBERLAIN-KING

BLACKSTAFF PRESS

First published in 2015
by Blackstaff Press
4D Weavers Court
Linfield Road
Belfast BT12 5GH

Design by Lisa Dynan
Illustrations by Samara Leibner at www.samaraleibner.com,
except where indicated

Reggie Chamberlain-King has asserted his right under the Copyright, Designs and
Patents Act to be identified as the editor of this work.

Printed and bound by CPI Group UK (Ltd), Croydon CR0 4YY

A CIP catalogue record for this book is available from the British Library

ISBN 978 0 85640 953 0

www.blackstaffpress.com

CONTENTS

For Carmel and Johnny

AN INTRODUCTION

The name of the old Viking settlement on the bay was derived from the tidal pool at Wood Quay: the Dark – or Black – Pool, *an Dubh Linn*, where the Poddle joins the Liffey. It is fitting that Dublin should be named for this reservoir of water, its still surface, and the black, obscured life underneath, as there is always something dark beneath the surface of the city. Those with a mischievous eye may even see, in the Scandinavian and Celtic names for the place – Dyflin, Dyflinn, Divlyn – the Devil hidden there. Certainly, strange things happen when lines cross, rivers meet, and roads fork.

From that Viking landing onward, there have been many histories of Dublin: its political story; its social past; its topographical and geographical changes. It is a place that has been well mapped out. This book is not about those things though; it is about the things that are not fit for such histories: the minutiae, the grace notes, the deviations, and the inconsistencies. It is a map of the city where all the streets turn into cul-de-sacs; that is, each story is a tangent or a run-off. The only way back to the main thoroughfares and avenues is to return the way you came.

The Weird is that which runs counter to expectation. It is necessarily small. The Weird can be an incident, an accident, an action, or a way of being. It fills you with giddy delight or horror, because it exists at the extremes and at the edges. That doesn't mean that the Weird is not part of life, just that it is not part of the narrative. It is not the big picture, but the big picture, when one moves close enough, is composed of much smaller, stranger images.

This book is made up of such small things: newspaper clippings;

incidental notes; extracts from centuries-old guidebooks; letters and accounts. It is a map drawn up in a darkened room, under the shadow of towering piles of periodicals and stacks of old volumes; it is not a map charted on foot. It is a miscellany.

And Dublin is a miscellany too. It is its own collection of disparate elements, sitting side by side. As a child, on a train approaching Connolly, on my first visits here, I would see stretches of sand give way to red-brick then to white Georgian lattices. We would visit some friend in the suburbs, pass Victorian buildings, stroll down medieval walkways, and lean on a plaque that bore the name of some revolutionary hero. This whole was Dublin, but no one part of it was Dublin.

What appears in this volume, then, is that which I have chosen. That is the only criterion any piece was required to meet for inclusion. The thesis of the book only took form once the book was finished and that form is the book itself. For example, it was on the second proof read that I noticed two Dubliners named Gannon took their own lives in ghastly circumstances in 1881, the first in New York on page 110, the other at the Grand Canal on page 152. Further research may conclude coincidence or family trait, but, for the purposes of the Weird, they are as closely related to one another as they are to the Monstrous Kitten on page 64 and the Messianic Prophet on page 131. The reach of Weird Dublin is far and wide, but its grip is light.

Perhaps this is a map, then, where all the roads are implied; no connection between A and B is drawn in heavy pencil. But one can always draw in those roads oneself or, if you are brave enough, walk them.

RCK

ENTER
STAGE
RIGHT

Three wooden devices were invented, wrote Dean Swift, to raise a man over other men: the pulpit, the gallows, and the stage.

To the Dubliner, the stage is highest of them all. It is both gibbet and lectern, both sacred and criminal. There is the Abbey and there is the gallows gate. And a playwright must be a sinner before becoming a saint. Everybody knows that.

Those who have the added pleasure of knowing actors, however, will be aware that that merry band don't always require a stage to think themselves higher than other people.

MONSTER SALOON,

CRAMPTON COURT, DAME-STREET,

CROWDED NIGHTLY WITH THE ELITE OF SOCIETY.

ENGAGEMENT EXTRAORDINARY OF
MR. AND MRS. HARRISON IN
THE TERRIFIC COMBATS
WITH THEIR WONDERFUL
NEWFOUNDLAND DOGS!

ENTHUSIASTIC RECEPTION OF
YANKEE SMITH;
LOUD APPLAUSE OF
MISS BEAUCHAMP,
the celebrated Serio-Comic Singer;

DECIDED HIT OF
MR. BISHOP,
*the eminent Scottish Vocalist, who will appear
in his splendid Native Costume;*

IMMENSE APPROBATION OF
MISS ANNIE EARLE,
the Sentimental Vocalist;

GREAT EXCITEMENT CREATED BY
THE BROTHERS CARR
in their pleasing entertainment

FINE WINES, BRANDIES, &C., KIDNEYS AND OYSTERS.

MR. GALLAHER IN HIS VARIOUS CHARACTERS.

Patrick Frederick Gallaher (1800–1863) was the most acclaimed ventriloquist in Ireland in the Victorian era, loved widely for his wit and trickery. Born in Chapelizod, he lived in Dublin and Cork both, while touring across the country and England. Although educated for the priesthood, he instead dedicated his life to bamboozling the Irish public through stagecraft, extravagant costumes and putting words in people's mouths.

THE DEAD ALIVE!

One Sunday night, Mr. Gallaher the celebrated ventriloquist observed two simple country-looking fellows carrying a coffin out to Roundtown. When they got near to the bridge at Harold's-cross, they stopped to rest themselves.

Mr. Gallaher pretended to be walking quietly by them, when he threw his voice into the coffin and immediately a loud shriek of agony was heard to issue, followed by cries of "Oh! Murther! Murther! Is it the canal you're going to throw me in?"

"Oh! Good Christians," cried a poor woman who was attracted by the noise, "here's a dead man in the coffin that wants to fight his two murderers." A crowd was immediately collected, the two poor countrymen were arrested as resurrectionists, and it was not until the coffin was opened and examined that they were permitted to proceed with their burden.

Just as the crowd was dispersing, a voice from the coffin was heard to exclaim, "Now boys, after all the trouble I gave you, I hope you won't forget to bury me dacently".

London Pioneer
November 11th, 1847

Gallaher passed away at the age of sixty-three, after a short illness. Three years earlier, his son, John Blake Gallaher, had become editor of the *Freeman's Journal*, where the following obituary appeared.

GALLAHER – April 7, in Amiens-street, Dublin, aged 63, Mr. P.F. Gallaher, the celebrated ventriloquist. He passed out of the world in peace with God and with all mankind, on Monday night, in the sixty-third year of his age. He acted his part well "off" as well as on the stage and, for many a long year, he shall be spoken of with kind regret and affectionate remembrance by the many whom he relieved in their want and suffering and by a circle of friends to whom his genuine good qualities had endeared him.

Freeman's Journal
April 9th, 1863

—— MR. GARBUT AND COMPANION ——

A curious occurrence took place, at a tavern, last week between Mr. Garbut, the Ventriloquist, and one of the waiters. The former called for dinner, which was served up, and he placed at the table with him his little puppet, Tommy, with which it would seem he converses, the oddity of which not a little surprised the waiter. Mr. Garbut having dined, he rang the bell and, the attendant appearing, Tommy, as was imagined, demanded what was to pay. This so frightened the boy, who could not observe the ventriloquist speaking, that he ran downstairs and swore he would not receive the reckoning in the room he came from, for he was sure the two that were in it were the Devil and some conjurer and, had the Ventriloquist thought proper, he might have come off with dining for nothing, during the consternation the waiter created in the house.

Freeman's Journal
January 23rd, 1798

THE THEATRE IN DUBLIN

It was rather astonishing to see what they would put up with. One of the turns was a conjuror, a Jew-boy with a Cockney accent – very nervous and, at the same time, very pert, who poured out a flood of stale patter while he drew eggs out of a top hat, removed fowls from a kettle, and, laying a red handkerchief over an empty tumbler, removed the handkerchief and displayed the tumbler full of water.

The audience bore with him with patience and, when, as the grand finale to his performance, he fired a pistol and caused a huge green flag with the harp of Erin on it to flutter down across the stage, he created a positive "furor." The cheering went on interminably, while the Jew-boy, "proud no doubt" of "all the Irish blood in him," stood bowing and smirking in the middle of the stage.

I came away from the theatre feeling that Irish audiences must be exceptionally good-natured and easy to please.

Dublin Explorations and Reflections by an Englishman
1917

ROTUNDO--ROBERT HOUDIN

There is an ease, an elegance and lightness about the performances of Robert Houdin unapproached altogether by any other professors of the magic art. In his empty hand, he produces a crystal ball – he divides this before your eyes into two crystal balls each as large as the first, and then makes them disappear. He gives a lady or gentleman a card and an empty box, turns to the stage and tells her to put the card in the box and shut it – he produces the card on the stage and on the box being opened five yards away from him there is a canary bird in it. He brings in an ordinary portfolio and places it on two skeleton supporters; from this he brings out, first drawings--then two elegant Paris bonnets which should have been crushed to bits in the space assigned to them--then three large stew-pans, one of them blazing on fire, another holding water to put out the fire! and, at the end of all, he brings out of his marvellous portfolio a large-sized bird-cage with a canary in it! His experiment about the box is the most singular and exciting of any of the tricks, but is too long for telling. He it was who first gave to the world the celebrated trick of "Ærial Suspension" and the "Inexhaustible Bottle." In short, in invention, ingenuity, and all other qualities necessary, he is the very prince of conjurors and wizards.

Freeman's Journal
March 18th, 1852

M. Houdin, in his prime, after whom
Harry Houdini took his stage name

MAGIC WONDERS
ROTUNDO
ROBERT HOUDIN, OF PARIS
The Celebrated Conjuror
Who had the honour of performing before
HER MAJESTY THE QUEEN,
The Royal Family,
And the Nobility in the United Kingdom,
Continues to give his
SOIREES FANTASTIQUES and **MAGICAL ILLUSIONS**
EVERY EVENING

The tricks and transformations are all his own inventions, and the astonishing Automatons made by himself have procured him several National Medals as rewards of merit for these surprising Works of Art.

Premiere Seats (Reserved)	...	...	3s
Second Seats	...	...	2s
Back Seats	...	...	1s

Children admitted Half Price to the Reserved and Second Seats only.

Tickets and seats may be reserved at the Concert Room, Rotunda, daily, from 12 to 4 o'Clock, at Robinson and Bursell's, and at all the Music Sellers.

Doors open at half-past Seven, commence at Eight o'Clock, and terminate at Ten.

DUBLIN THEATRE SENSATION

In the course of the performance of what has been advertised as "The Dublin Revue," there is a ballet. The story of the ballet is built around an obstreperous goat, which earns the reputation among the simpler rural folk of being possessed of an evil spirit. The goat is exorcised and the evil spirit is expelled, after much weird gesticulating by the "priest," attired, by the way, in the usual stage-clergyman style. The exorcist is accompanied by an acolyte, bearing a tray, on which there is a lighted candle, a bell, and a book.

The *Catholic Press*, Australia
June 11th, 1931

NOTED DESTRUCTION TO DUBLIN THEATRES AND PICTURE HOUSES

Theatre Royal	1880	Fire
Theatre Royal	1912	Fire
Empire Theatre	1913	Bomb
Masterpiece Cinema	1925	Landmine
Savoy Cinema	1934	Stormed by Youths
Dublin Picture House	1935	Bomb
Bohemian Picture House, Philsboro	1935	Bomb
Carlton Cinema, O'Connell Street	1947	Letter bomb
Abbey Theatre	1951	Fire

FELL DEAD AS THEY CHEERED
STAGE TRAGEDY AT DUBLIN THEATRE

For the second time in four months, the Gaiety Theatre in Dublin was the setting for real tragedy recently. But the audience did not know ... The show went on.

Mrs. Zena Carroll, aged 35, of Brixton, London, a leading member of the pantomime "Dick Whittington," had just made her exit and the audience was still cheering her when she fell dead in the wings.

She was taken to hospital, still in her pantomime dress, and the performance proceeded.

"Some of the girls in the chorus wept before going on again," a member of the cast told a "Daily Mail" reporter, "but they played their parts so well that the audience did not suspect that anything unusual had happened."

Last September, a young woman member of a wedding party was fatally burned when her dress caught fire and she jumped, screaming, from her box into the auditorium of the same theatre.

Tweed Daily, Australia
March 30th, 1937

ALAS! POOR EDWIN!

The melancholy and sudden death of this excellent Comedian, which took place yesterday morning, is not only a loss to the Stage, but society at large, of which he was a pleasant and most worthy member.

As a compliment to his memory, Mr. Jones, with great humanity, shut the Theatre last night from any performance, conscious that E's brother Actors, who held him in great esteem, and particularly his amiable and disconsolate widow, would be unequal to any dramatic appearance. It is said, in the Green-room and in his own family, that his nerves have been in a state of great agitation since the illiberal and unjust attack made on his professional character by the Familiar Epistles; and we may believe that a man who had, for many years, been a favourite on the English Stage and who exerted himself with some reputation to please an Irish audience, must have felt some irritation and pain of mind at meeting with such ridicule from an anonymous writer and those feelings might have hastened his exit from the stage of life.

If so, let the author of the Familiar Epistles triumph in the calamity he has made and in the barbarity of productions so severe and illiberal against the performers of the Irish Stage.

Freeman's Journal
February 23rd, 1832

FAREWELL TO EDWIN

The remains of the unfortunate Mr. Edwin, the Comedian, were interred on Sunday morning last, in the burial-ground of St. Bridget's parish. They were attended to the grave by all his

Thespian brethren and a number of respectable citizens.

Mrs. Edwin has been, with much good nature, invited by Mr. Jones, the proprietor of the Theatre, to spend some time at his country residence to soothe her lamentable affliction.

Freeman's Journal
February 26th, 1832

S t. Werburgh's Church – Edwin the player is likewise interred here; and, on the tomb marking his place of rest, a bitter reproach is engraved against the author of the Familiar Epistles, the severity of which is stated to have caused his premature death.

The Picture of Dublin: or, Stranger's Guide to the Irish Metropolis
William Curry
1835

∽ PADDY'S DESCRIPTION OF PIZARRO ∽ A BALLAD
Generally attributed to John Edwin

From the county of Monaghan, lately I came!
The harvest to reap, Master Doody's my name.

My cousin Shaughnossy I met t'other day!
Says he, won't you go to the Drury-lane play?
Tol de rol la, Tol de rol la ra la,
Tol rol la ra la, la ra la, la.
I'st the play that you mean? – Arrah, Doody you're right,
Where they treat the whole Town with Pizarro tonight.
Och! says I, if they treat me, the thing's nate and clean,
But the treat, as he call'd it, cost me a Thirteen.

The great green thing drew up and a lady I spy'd;
A man came to kiss her, she scornfully cry'd--
Get out you blackguard or I'll bodder your gig;
Then in came Pizarro, who growl'd like a pig.

In the days of Old Goree, a long time ago,
The Spaniards all march'd to Peru, you must know;
Saying, Give us your jewels, your cash, and your keys,

But a man they call'd Rolla, said, No, if you please.
This Rolla a star in the day-time appear'd
And, in a long speech, he the soldiers thus cheer'd,
Saying--Lather the dons, you must do the nate thing,
For who wou'd not die for their country and king?

Then Och! what a hubbub, confusion and strife!
And Rolla, God bless him! he sav'd the King's life:
The went to Alonzo, coop'd up in a jail
And sending him off, staid himself in for bail.

Then Pizarro came forward and, with a gossoon,
Which was handled by Rolla as I would a spoon--
But as he was scaling a bridge o'er the greens
He was shot by a rogue from behind all the screens.

The Rolla came running and with him the child
And he look'd all the world just as if he was wild;
Saying--Take the dear creature, it's my blood that's spilt,
In defence of your child, blood and ouns, how I'm kilt!

Then Alonzo gave Paddy Pizarro a bow
Which laid him as dead as Old Bryan Barrow*;
And poor Rolla's body was laid out in state
And twenty fair virgins all join'd at his wake.

Then Alonzo came forward and handsomely bow'd
Saying--Ladies and Gentleman (meaning the crowd),
All with your permission to-morrow night then,
We'll murder Pizarro all over again.

DEAF BUT NOT DUMB

Strange as it may seem, one of the most effective comedians of the present day is so deaf that he cannot hear the other actors playing with him on the stage. Such is his experience of stage business and so thoroughly does he study all the parts of every piece in which he plays, as well as the peculiar movements and countenances of the different performers concerned, that he never makes a mistake relative to the proper time of speaking and what he ought to say.

Irish Times
October 1st, 1863

---

*   Brian Boru

ROYAL SPORT OF COCK-FIGHTING

ON MONDAY, the 25th of FEBRUARY, the first of the Septenial Mains between the Gentlemen of the KING'S COUNTY and the Gentlemen of the COUNTY of FERMANAGH, for TWENTY GUINEAS a Battle, and FIVE HUNDRED the Main or Odd Battle, begin fighting at the New Pit, Farmers' Repository, Stephen's-green.

The Noblemen and Gentlemen Members of the Sod and Jockey Club, intend dining at Falkener's Tavern, Dawson-street, each Day, and for that Week the Club will be open to all Gentlemen Sportsmen that wish to join in the amusement, provided that they are introduced by a Member.

The Gentlemen who intend to Dine will please so leave their name at the Bar.

Freeman's Journal, Feb 1805

NEW THEATRE ROYAL
ABBEY STREET
FOR SIX NIGHTS ONLY
THE GREATEST WONDER OF THE AGE,
MONSIEUR CHYLINKSI
(late Lieutenant in the Rifle Brigade of Augustow, in Poland), who will make his first appearance on
MONDAY & TUESDAY, March 8th & 9th,
in his Chemico-Physical and Gymnastic Representations, in Four Characters, viz.,
THE ATHLETIC MAN! THE MODERN HERCULES!!
THE FIRE KING, AND THE POLISH SALAMANDER!!!

In the First Character of the ATHLETIC MAN, Monsieur Chylinski will exhibit a variety of Feats of Physical Force and prove that they may be gained by continual and persevering exercise, united to a knowledge of the Mechanical Structure of the Human Frame.

In the Second Character, as the MODERN HERCULES, he will give several extraordinary examples of his great Strength and Gymnastical Exercises.

In the Third character of the FIRE KING, he will go through a variety of Chemical Experiments.

In the Fourth Character of the POLISH SALAMANDER, he will give a variety of astonishing proofs of his Incombustibility by a selection of Experiments.

—— A SELECTION OF ODD PLAYS ——

THE SHAM PRINCE; OR, NEWS FROM PASSAU. Comedy by Charles Shadwell, 1720. This play was written in five days and acted in Dublin, the design of it being to expose a public cheat, who had at that time passed himself on the Irish nation as a person of the first importance and, by that means, imposed on many to their great loss and injury. The scene is laid in Dublin and the time of action six hours.

THE ORATORS. Comedy of three acts by Samuel Foote, 1762. In order to point out the absurdities which are frequently run into both in the matter and manner of argumentation, Mr. Foote has thrown into his design a great variety of characters, some of which were supposed to be drawn from life; particularly, one of an eminent printer of a neighbouring kingdom who, with all the disadvantages of age, person, and address, and, even the deficiency of a leg, was perpetually assuming airs of the greatest importance, continually repeating stories of his wit; and, not content with being a most tiresome egotist in other respects, was even continually talking of his amours and boasting of being a favourite with the fair sex.

It may be observed, however, that George Faulkener, the printer, when Foote next arrived in Dublin, brought an action against him for a libel.

THE TRYAL OF SAMUEL FOOTE, ESQ. FOR A LIBEL ON PETER PARAGRAPH. Farce by Samuel Foote. The scene lies in the Four Courts, Dublin. Mr. Foote performed, first, the part of Counsellor Demur, supposed to be employed against him and, afterwards (slipping off the barrister's gown and wig), appeared as himself.

THE TRUE-BORN IRISHMAN. Farce by Charles Macklin. Acted at Dublin, 1763.*

THE TRUE-BORN SCOTCHMAN. Farce by Charles Macklin. Acted at Dublin, 1764. It was generally performed twice a week, during the season, to full and respectable audiences; and the character

---

* The first night of Macklin's *True-Born Irishman*, in Dublin, a well-known eccentric gentleman, who had just come to a great fortune, sat with a large party in the stage box. When Massink came on as Pat Fitz Mongrel, this said gentleman in the boxes cried out, "What, that's me! but what sort of rascally coat is that they've dressed me in? – here, I'll dress you!" He stood up, took off his own rich gold-laced coat and flung it on the stage. Massink took it up smiling, stepped to the wing, threw off his own, and returned upon the stage in the gentleman's fine coat which produced the greatest applause and pleasure among the audience.

Dublin Theatres and Theatre Customs (1637–1820)
La Tourette Stockwell
1938

of Sir Pertinax Mac Sycophant was thought so strong a picture of a Scotchman that Macklin is said to have received a note from a young Scotch nobleman, then in high favour at the Castle, accompanied with a suit of handsome laced dress clothes, saying "that he begged his acceptance of that present, as a small mark of the pleasure he received from the exhibition of so fine a picture of his grandfather."

THE NEW WONDER: A WOMAN HOLDS HER TONGUE. Farce by W.C. Oulton. Acted at Capel Street, Dublin, 1784.

THE MAD-HOUSE. Musical Entertainment by W.C. Oulton. Acted in Dublin, 1785.

THE STONE-EATER by C. Stuart. A piece of contemporary nonsense, 1788. Holdfast, believing in the prediction of a fortune-teller, thinks that his daughter is destined to marry a stone-eater and is happy in the idea that his son-in-law can be so cheaply provided for. Captain O'Thunder was born at Stoney Batter and has lived by the Black Rock, near Dublin; this, the old man fancies, must be the stone-eater: but Captain Leek was born in Flintshire; and this must be another stone-eater. To decide between them, a collation of marble is ordered; and by such mummery did the piece obtain "universal applause."

THE VILLAGE LAWYER. Farce, 1795. The theatre manager was ignorant of the author, who, as reported, was a dissenting minister in Dublin, but, on account of his situation, did not choose to avow it. It was even put into Mr. Colman's hand, without the author's knowledge, by a friend who had very fortunately saved the MS. from the flames; for, like the manager, the author himself was apprehensive it would not do on the English stage; he was, however, agreeably surprised when not only informed of its great success, but likewise presented with the emolument arising from the farce.

Some entries from: *Biographica Dramatica*; *Or a Companion to the Playhouse*, compiled by David Erskine Baker, Isaac Reed, and Stephen Jones, 1811

GREAT SUCCESS

The Inhabitants of Dublin and its vicinity are respectfully informed that the Exhibition of the Devonshire Giant, Welch Dwarf, White Negro, large Serpents, Crocodile, Armadillo, &c., will still remain open each day during the week, from Eleven o'clock in the Morning, until Ten in the Evening, at 23, CAPEL-STREET. It is desired, by many of the Nobility and Gentry that witnessed the great Boa constrictor Serpent fed on Wednesday last, that the Anaconda will be fed on This Day (Monday), the 1st of March, at half-past two o'clock. Admission to witness this novelty—Ladies and Gentlemen 1s.; Servants and Children 6d. each; and, if the Serpent does not feed, the proprietor will return the money.

Freeman's Journal
March 1st, 1841

OWEN FARRELL

An Irish dwarf, who, in 1716, was footman to a colonel in Dublin. He was 3ft 9in in height, but very heavily, though clumsily, made, and his strength was amazing. He could carry four men at one time, two of them sitting astride on each of his extended arms. After exhibiting himself as a show in Ireland, he came to London, where, being too lazy to work, he got a living by begging in the streets. He sold the reversion of his body, in consideration of a small weekly allowance of money, to a London surgeon, who, after the dwarf's death, made a skeleton of his bones, which, we believe, is still preserved in the collection of William Hunter at Glasgow.

Bacchus Marsh Express, Australia
March 22nd, 1890

A GLASSOPHONE

An Irishman named Richard Pockrich (I never heard the name before) played on 'Musical Glasses' in Dublin, in 1743. The idea was to fill a set of tumblers (drinking glasses) with water and then friction the edges with the hand and soft musical sounds would be produced. The note depends on how much water you have in the glass. You have there music by friction. The Irishman who formulated the idea and made music with the glasses created quite a furore and went over to London the next year.

Sydney Stock and Station Journal
April 29th, 1921

Samara Leibner

He was the true inventor of the musical glasses, which attracted the attention of Mozart, Gluck, and other composers, and was, afterwards, perfected by Franklin. Pockrich made a considerable income by his performances on the glasses in England and Ireland and it was while on one of his tours that he met his death, being burned by a fire which broke out in his room in Hamlin's coffee-house, Sweeting's Alley, near the Royal Exchange, London, in the year 1759.

The Poets of Ireland
David O'Donoghue
1893

Richard Pockrich (*c*.1690–1759) preferred the title 'Captain' Pockrich, which it seems he never earned. Born in County Monaghan, he inherited a fortune that was quickly dissipated across various eccentric schemes, of which the Glass Armonica was not the most outlandish.

His life's work included:

- An attempt to reclaim the bogs of Ireland by draining them and planting vineyards in their place.
- Plans for an orchestra of drums, totalling twenty in number, all of different sizes and timbres. The pieces would be performed by one player, in the centre of the

instruments, striking the drums with a staff.

- The manufacture and provision of wings for the time in the future when people would be able to fly rather than walk.

- Running for parliament on two occasions, hoping to represent first Monaghan, then Dublin; and failing both times.

- Hoping to increase human longevity exponentially through a lifelong cycle of blood transfusions.

The musical glasses were his only success and these, even, came quickly on the heels of failure, Pockrich having established a substandard brewery on his arrival in Dublin in 1715.

Mr. Pockrich, in his brewery near Island-bridge, happening one day to be seized by bailiffs, thus addressed them: "Gentlemen, I am your prisoner, but before I do myself the honour to attend you, give me leave, as an humble performer of musick, to entertain you with a tune." "Sir," replies one of the bailiffs, "we come here to execute our warrant, not to hear tunes." "Gentlemen," says the Captain, "I submit to your authority, but in the interim, while you are only taking a dram ... Here Jack!" calling to his servant, "bring a bottle of the Ros Solis I lately distilled: I say, Gentlemen, before you take a dram I shall dispatch my tune." In the meantime, he flourishes a prelude on the glasses and afterwards displays his skill through all the pleasing turns and variations of the 'Black Joke'. The monsters, charmed with the magick of his sounds, for some time stand at gaze. At length, recovering from their trance, they accost the Captain: "Sir, upon your parole of honour to keep the secret, we give you your liberty." "Tis well, playing upon the glasses is not more common: if it were, I believe our trade would find little employment."

Essays, Poetical, Moral, &c.
Thomas Newburgh
1769

THE PIG-FACED LADY

For oral relations of the pig-faced lady, we must go to Dublin. If we make inquiries there respecting her, we shall be shewn the hospital that was founded on her account. We will be told that her picture and silver trough are to be seen in the building and that she was christened Grisly, on account of her hideous appearance. Any further doubts, after receiving this information, will be considered as insults to common sense. Now, the history of Steevens's Hospital, the institution referred to, is simply this: In 1710, Dr. Steevens, a benevolent physician, bequeathed his real estate, producing £650 per annum to his only sister, Griselda, during her life; and, after her death, vested it in trustees for the erection and endowment of a hospital. Miss Steevens, being a lady of active benevolence – a very unusual character in those days, though happily not an uncommon one now – determined to build the hospital in her lifetime. Devoting £450 of her income to this purpose, she collected subscriptions and donations and, by dint of unceasing exertion, succeeded, in a few years, in opening a part of the building equal to the accommodation of forty patients. Whether it was the uncommon name of Griselda or the unccommon benevolence of this lady that gave rise to the vulgar notion respecting her face will probably be never satisfactorily explained. But her portrait hangs in the library of the hospital, proving her to have been a very pleasant-looking-lady, with a peculiarly benevolent cast of countenance.

A lady, to whom the writer applied for information, thus writes from Dublin: "The idea that Miss Steevens was a pig-faced lady still prevails among the vulgar; when I was young, everybody believed it. When this century was in its teens, it was customary, in genteel society, for parties to be made up to go to the hospital, to see the silver trough and pig-faced picture. The matron, or housekeeper, that shewed the establishment, never denied the existence of those curiosities, but always alleged she could not shew them, implying, by her mode of saying it, that she dared not, that to do so would be contrary to the stringent orders she received. The housekeeper, no doubt, obtained many shillings and tenpennies by this equivocating mode of keeping up the delusion. Besides, many persons who had gone to the hospital to see the trough and picture did not like to acknowledge that they had not seen them."

The Book of Days, Vol. 2
Robert Chambers
1864

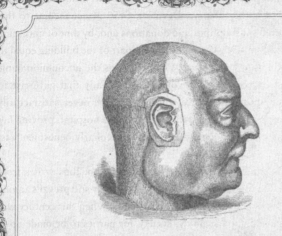

The
DEAN'S
SKULL

The house in Hoey's Alley in which Swift was born

THE DEAN DIES

Last Saturday, at three o'clock in the afternoon, died that great and eminent patriot, the Rev. Dr. Jonathan Swift, Dean of St. Patrick's, Dublin, in the seventy-eighth year of his age; who was born in the parish of St. Werburgh's, Dublin, the 30th of November, 1667, at his uncle, Counsellor Godwin Swift's house, in Hoey's Alley, which in those times was the general residence of the chief lawyers. His genius, works, learning, and charity are so universally admired that, for a newswriter to attempt his character would be the highest presumption; yet as the printer hereof is proud to acknowledge his infinite obligations to that prodigy of wit, he can only lament that he is by no means equal to so bold an undertaking.

Faulkner's Dublin Journal
October 22nd, 1745

A MELANCHOLY SPECTACLE

A person who resides in my family is one of the few persons, perhaps the only one now living, who witnessed this melancholy spectacle. She remembers him as well as if it was but yesterday: he was laid out in his own hall and great crowds went to see him. His coffin was open; he had on his head neither cap nor wig; there was not much hair on the front or very top, but it was long and thick behind, very white, and was like flax on the pillow. Mrs. Barnard, his nursetender, sat at his head; but having occasion to leave the room for a short time, some person cut a lock of hair from his head, which she missed upon her return, and, after that day, no person was admitted to see him.

William M. Mason
1820

ITEM: I give and bequeath to my Executors all my worldly Substance, of what Nature or Kind soever for the following Uses and Purposes, that is to say, to the Intent that they, or the Survivors or Survivor of them, his Executors, or Administrators, as soon as conveniently may be after my Death, shall turn it all into ready Money, and lay out the same in purchasing Lands of Inheritance in Fee-simple, situate in any

Province of Ireland, except Connaught, but as near to the City of
Dublin, as conveniently can be found(...). That the Profits shall be laid
out in purchasing a Piece of Land laid out for this charitable Purpose
by the Governors of Dr. Steeven's Hospital, agreeable to the Dean's
Desire in his Life-time Land, situated near Dr. Steeven's Hospital, or if
it cannot be there had, somewhere in or near the City of Dublin, large
enough for the Purposes herein after mentioned, and in building thereon
an Hospital large enough for the Reception of as many Idiots and
Lunaticks as the annual Income of the said Lands and worldly Substance
shall be sufficient to maintain. And, I desire that the said Hospital may
be called St. Patrick's Hospital(...) And my further Will and Desire is
that, when the said Hospital shall be built, the whole yearly Income of
the said Lands and Estate, shall, for ever after, be laid out in providing
Victuals, Cloathing, Medicines, Attendance, and all other Necessaries
for such Idiots and Lunaticks, as shall be received into the same. And,
if a sufficient Number of Idiots and Lunaticks, cannot readily be found,
I desire that Incurables may be taken into the said Hospital to supply
such Deficiency: But that no Person shall be admitted into it that labours
under any infectious Disease: And that all such Idiots, Lunaticks and
Incurables, as shall be received into the said Hospital, shall constantly
live and reside therein, as well in the Night as in the Day.

The Last Will and Testament of Jonathan Swift
1745

VERSES ON THE DEATH OF DR. SWIFT

"He gave the little wealth he had
To build a house for fools and mad;
And showed by one satiric touch,
No nation wanted it so much."

Jonathan Swift
1739

"The Dean must die!—our idiots to maintain!
Perish ye idiots! and long live the Dean!"

Gentleman's Monthly Intelligencer
January 1735

It has been supposed by his biographers that a presentiment of his insanity induced the Dean to devote his fortune to the erection of a lunatic asylum; and probably from an expression in Orrery's* work, that he was a fit inmate for his own asylum, it is generally believed that Swift was the first patient in the hospital, although it was not erected till several years after his death.

The Closing Years of Dean Swift's Life with Remarks on Stella
Dr. William R. Wilde, M.R.I.A., F.R.C.S.**
1849

For some years past he has been entirely deprived of memory and by degrees fell into a perfect insensibility.

Dublin Courant
October 23rd, 1745

---

* John Boyle, 5th Earl of Cork and 5th Earl of Orrery, F.R.S.

** Father of Oscar Wilde

AN EXAMINATION OF THE TIME

The Rev. David Stevens, one of the Dean's Chapter, had, it is related, several times expressed a desire to his friends and physicians, that the Dean should be trepanned*, from an opinion which entertained that he laboured under water on the brain; and to a certain degree his diagnosis proved correct.

A post mortem examination was made by Mr. Whiteway, his relative, but all we are able to learn is, "that he opened the skull, and found much water in the brain." Dr. Lyon, revising the work from which this is quoted, has altered the expression to "the sinus of his brain being loaded with water." What other pathological appearances presented at the autopsy it is now difficult to say. Thus passed from amongst us one of the brightest ornaments of our country and the greatest genius of his age.

*

Before we enter upon the consideration of those most interesting inquiries, we beg to lay before our readers the following account of the SECOND post mortem examination of the Dean's head, on its exhumation in 1835.

The circumstance becoming known to a few scientific gentlemen in this city, several persons were present at the disinterment and, among the rest, the late Dr. Houston, who has given the following interesting account of what took place.

The Closing Years of Dean Swift's Life with Remarks on Stella
Dr. William R. Wilde, M.R.I.A., F.R.C.S.
1849

ON THE AUTHENTICITY OF THE SKULLS OF DEAN SWIFT
AND STELLA BY DR. HOUSTON OF DUBLIN

To George Combe, Esq.
Dublin, October 22, 1835

Dear Sir,

In compliance with your request, as conveyed to me by Mr. Carmichael, I beg leave to forward you some memoranda relative to the disinterment of the skulls of the celebrated

---

*   Dean Swift, of course, needed trepanation like he needed a hole in the head. However, archaeological evidence of trepanation in Medieval Ireland has been found, including one skull recovered from the cemetery at the site of St. Stephen's Hospital, now occupied by Mercer's Medical Centre. In this instance, it is believed that the patient survived the procedure.

George Combe

St Patrick's Cathedral

Dean Swift and his favourite Stella*, which may serve to remove any doubts as to the genuineness of these relics. I am still farther prompted to acquiesce in your request, by a desire to remove some prejudices, to which an imperfect acquaintance with the facts leading to their disinterment appears to have given rise; particularly on account of the feelings of the present venerable Dean of St. Patrick's, by whose permission I was enabled to take advantage of an unavoidable temporary exposure of the coffins in which they lay entombed. It was no idle curiosity, neither can we boast of its being zeal for the cause of science, which led to the disinterment; it was purely a matter of accident. In making some alterations in the aisle of the church, it became necessary to expose several coffins** and, amongst others, those of Swift and Stella, which lay side by side; and I would ask the most sensitive on such matters, 'What aggravation of the exposure was it to transfer for a few hours,

---

* Esther Johnson (1681-1728), a close friend of Swift, whose supposed marriage to the dean remains either a secret or a myth.

** "After the beginning of the last century, "the frequency of floods in the Poddle river, and insufficiency of sewers to carry off the superabundant water, was the occasion of much injury," to St. Patrick's Cathedral, "and moreover rendered it, on account of damp, unsafe to assemble in." Now one of the last public acts of the Dean, before his illness, was having measures taken by the Chapter to prevent this dampness and these inundations; and it is remarkable that their continuance in the year 1835 was the cause of his remains being disturbed. The repairs then necessary were, we are happy to add, the sole cause of these sacred relics being again exposed."

from the hands of common workmen to those of persons capable of appreciating the value of such objects, the time-worn bones of the great deceased?'

The coffin lay about two feet and a half below the flags; it was surrounded by wet clay, and nearly filled inside with water. The workmen having arrived at this stage of the disinterment, exhibited the utmost curiosity and haste to determine the truth of a tradition handed down to them by old Brennan*, namely, that the head of the Dean had been trepanned after his death, and before being laid in the grave. Brennan's oft-repeated story was that, in consequence of the state of his master's intellects for a long time previous to death, the surgeons had opened his head to ascertain the cause of his insanity. He boasted that he himself had been present at the operation, and that he even held the basin in which the brain was placed after its removal from the skull. He told, moreover, that there was brain mixed with water to such an amount as to fill the basin and, by their quantity, to call forth expressions of astonishment from the medical gentlemen engaged in the examination. The curiosity of the workmen was excited only with a view to determine the truth or falsehood of Brennan's story. But the suspense was not of long duration: as soon as the coffin was sufficiently emptied of the water to yield a view of the bones, which lay at the bottom, a general exclamation burst forth that "Old Brennan had spoken truth;" for the top of the skull was discovered lying alongside the bottom part, from which it had been detached horizontally by a saw.

All the bones of the skeleton lay in the position into which they had fallen when deprived of the flesh that enveloped and held them together. The skull, with the calvarium by its side, lay at the top of the coffin; the bones of the neck lay next and, mixed with them were found the cartilages of the larynx, which by age had been converted into bone**. All the rings of the trachea, which had undergone the same change, were equally in a state of preservation and order. The dorsal vertebrae and ribs occupied the middle of the coffin; the bones of the arms and hands lay, as they had been placed in death, along the sides; and the pelvis and lower extremities were found towards the bottom. The

---

*   Richard Brennan, Dean Swift's faithful manservant and, latterly, beadle of St. Patrick's Cathedral.

** According to Dr. Wilde: "The only portion not returned (to the cathedral) was the larynx, the ossified fragments of which were abstracted by a bystander, a countryman of Swift's, and are now, we believe, in the city of New York, U.S."

teeth were nearly all gone and their sockets were filled up with bone. The whole were evidently the remains of a very aged man.

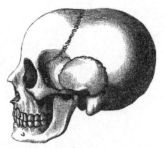
Stella's skull

There being no longer any doubt that the body which lay in this coffin was that of Doctor Swift, particular attention was paid to the examination of the bones of the neck and that part of the skull to which the first is articulated, in order to be certain that the head in the coffin really belonged to the other bones and that no question, founded on the possibility of a theft on the skull having been committed by the medical gentlemen who examined the body after death, should hereafter be raised; and it was evident to all persons present, among whom were several medical gentlemen of eminence, that the adaptation of the respective vertebrae to each other and of the first to the condyles of the occiput, was so perfect, that no doubt whatever of their all having belonged to the same individual could be entertained. They were all the bones of one man, and that, beyond all manner of doubt, the immortal Swift.

I beg leave, in conclusion, to say, that I have forwarded to you three casts of these heads, taken under my own inspection, and which I take the liberty of requesting you will present to the Phrenological Society of Edinburgh. The skull of the Dean having been found open in the coffin, I was enabled to have a cast of the inside taken, without doing violence to so sacred a relic: that of Stella being entire, I did not wish to wound public prejudice by inflicting on the head that injury which would have been necessary towards procuring a cast of its interior.

I remain, Dear Sir, your obedient Servant,

J. Houston.

Phrenological Journal and Miscellany
Volume 9, September 1834–March 1836

A MODEST PERUSAL

During the week or ten days which elapsed before they were returned (for returned they certainly were) they were carried to most of the learned, as well as all the fashionable societies of Dublin. The University,

Dr. William Wilde

where Swift had so often toiled, again beheld him, but in another phase; the Cathedral which heard his preaching, the Chapter-house which echoed his sarcasm, the Deanery which resounded with his sparking wit, and where he gossiped with Sheridan and Delany, the lanes and alleys which knew his charity, the squares and streets where the people shouted his name in the days of his unexampled popularity, the mansions where he was the honoured and much-sought guest, perhaps the very rooms he had often visited, were again occupied by the dust of Swift!

While these skulls of Swift and Stella were going the rounds, casts and drawings of them were made, from which we now afford our readers the engravings which accompany this work. Moreover, that of the Dean was

also examined, with a view to the elucidation of the malady under which he
so long laboured, and of which he died.

The Closing Years of Dean Swift's Life with Remarks on Stella
Dr. William. R. Wilde, M.R.I.A., F.R.C.S.
1849

AN ACCOUNT OF A MEETING OF
THE DUBLIN PHRENOLOGICAL SOCIETY
17TH AUGUST 1835

Dr. Houston presented himself to the meeting, having the day
previously obtained the skulls of the celebrated Dean Swift and Mrs
Esther Johnson, better known by the appellation "Stella."

Dr. Evanson remarked that the bones of the anterior part of the
head were considerably thickened and the internal surface of the
skull did not exhibit those impressions of the convolutions which
are to be found in the healthy subject. It was also on record that,
after the skull had been opened, a quantity of water was found
suffused upon the brain. It was not fair to condemn the science if
this head were not found to give an idea of the Dean's character;
for Phrenology paid regard only to developments occurring in the
brain of a person in full health and vigour.

It was not fair (Captain Ross observed, in reference to the
skull of Dean Swift) to raise a discussion upon skulls either
aged or diseased.

A conversation took place in reference to a plaster cast, made from
a marble bust of Dean Swift, executed during his lifetime by an
artist named Cunningham; but as the artists of those days were
not accustomed to pay that attention to the developments of the
head which is now given, it was considered to be unimportant in
reference to the debateable ground in question.

Dr. Evanson gave a highly interesting lecture on the skull of
"Stella," shewing that it bore out all the characteristics of that
singular and gifted woman.

Phrenological Journal and Miscellany
Volume 9, September 1834–March 1836

ACCOUNT OF THE SCULL OF DEAN SWIFT, RECENTLY DISINTERRED AT DUBLIN
From No. XLV of the Edinburgh Phrenological Journal

The scull was found to present the following appearances. At the base—roughened in the sphenoidal region; the processes prominent and sharp-pointed. Some parts, in the occipital fossae, the super-orbitar plates, and other portions of the scull, were so thin as to be transparent. Above the frontal protuberances (in the region of Benevolence) the bone was thickened, apparently by a deposition of bony matter on its inner surface—making the inner surface at that part on both sides flat in place of concave, and smoother than the other parts; which was the more remarkable as the other portions of the scull were rather thin. The two hemispheres were regular and symmetrical. Dr. Houston (who dictated to Mr Combe the foregoing description of the scull, which was approved of by all the other gentlemen present) suggested that the extraordinary powers of mind which Swift exhibited on many occasions may have arisen from diseased activity (We dissent from this opinion, but have no room to state our reasons! — Ed.); and Dr. Harrison remarked that the appearances were such as he had observed in patients who had been affected with epileptic fits.

We can fancy the 'glorious triumph' the first blush of the facts will give our friends, the anti-phrenologists, and the delight with which they will hail a scull with small intellectual and large animal indications as that of the caustic and powerful Swift. But, as a triumph founded on error must of necessity be very short-lived, we advise them to make the most of it in the meantime; because, the more minutely the case is examined, the more completely will it be found to harmonize in all its features with the phrenological philosophy.

Our readers will recollect that, as the brain decreases in volume in old age, and the scull no longer indicates its form with certainty at the period of life, it is held by Gall and Spurzheim and all other phrenologists to be impossible to predicate from the inspection of the sculls of very aged persons what their talents and dispositions were at the time of vigorous maturity; and, consequently, although useful as illustrations, such cases are never considered admissible as proofs either for or against Phrenology. Applying this principle to the case of Dean Swift, who is known to have died in very advanced

Dean Swift's brain

William R. Wilde

age, from water on the brain, the effect of long-standing disease, the phrenologist would not hold himself warranted to infer, from the mere inspection of the scull, what had been the talents and disposition of its possessor in the prime of life.

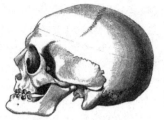

Dean Swift's skull

William R. Wilde

The brain is well known to decrease in volume and the scull to follow its shrinking surface, both in old age and in disease. In this instance, it was impossible to doubt that the brain had shrunk and that the inner table of the scull had followed it. If time and space permitted, we could adduce other examples of a similar nature.

We have much more to say, but our space is exhausted!

Phrenological Journal and Miscellany
Volume 9, September 1834–March 1836

A PHRENOLOGICAL EXAMINATION

We beg leave to premise that, prior to this date, a phrenological examination had been made by a distinguished professor of that ci-devant system, of a number of aged lunatics in the Richmond Asylum of this city, in which the previous characters of these persons was said to have been described from their cranioscopal examination, with great fidelity – a fact which was vauntingly proclaimed with no small degree of triumph by the advocates of that doctrine. Shortly afterwards, Swift's skull was handed to one of the great prophets of this art, who pronounced it to be a very commonplace skull indeed – nay, from the low frontal development, almost that of a fool; and in the measurements of the cranium given in the Phrenological Journal we find amativeness large and wit small! with similar contradictions to the well-known character of this great genius. But then, all these discrepancies are endeavoured to be accounted for by the fact that the skull then presented was not that of Swift the wit, the caustic writer, and the patriot, but that of Swift, the madman and the fool; and, to explain this, it has been asserted that the skull had collapsed or fallen in, in some places, during the period of his mental disease; although, in the previous instance to which we have alluded, at the Richmond Asylum, the periscope was made without taking into account this item in the physical as well as moral change of the lunatics.

Without examining into the arguments contained in the Phrenological

Journal, we at once deny the fact of Swift's skull having altered during life or of insanity ever producing the effects therein stated; and we may confidently defy its conductors to the proof. Esquirol,* one of the highest authorities on the subject, found, from a long series of careful observations, that the skull previously normal does not alter its form or capacity from long-constituted insanity or imbecility.

The Closing Years of Dean Swift's Life with Remarks on Stella
Dr. William R. Wilde, M.R.I.A., F.R.C.S.
1849

In a talk – 'Are the Phenomena of Mental Alienation consistent with the views regarding the Mental Faculties adopted by Phrenologists? – given to the Royal Medical Society, Edinburgh, on March 9th, 1837, Dr. David Skae, later resident physician of the Royal Edinburgh Asylum, compared the skulls of six great heroes with those of four notorious murderers: the latter included Haggart, McKaen, Pollard, and Lockey, while the former numbered Robert Burns, Jean de La Fontaine, Robert the Bruce, Héloïse, and, of course, Jonathan Swift and Stella. The personalities of these personages, it was hoped, were well known and Skae, then only a medical student, hoped to conclude the ongoing feud between pathology and phrenology then so heated.

The skulls were first measured with callipers and the capacity verified by immersion in water. "I assumed that the measurements of the crania thus calculated would correspond with the known characters of the individuals, if phrenology was true."

However, the results Skae found were "at variance with phrenology, and in many instances so utterly irreconcilable with its truth, as to appear altogether subversive of it." The casts were not the shapes they should be.

The response of the Phrenological community was, ironically, pathological: Skae's instruments were less nuanced than a skilled Phrenologist's seasoned fingers; his methodology was incompetent; and his measurements and results "entirely vitiate every conclusion to which they have been supposed to lead."

THE DIAGNOSIS

After the Dean's death, and subsequently to the post mortem examination, a plaster mask was taken from his face, and from this a bust was made, which is now in the Museum of the University, and which, notwithstanding its possessing much of the cadaverous appearance, is, we are strongly

---

* Early-nineteenth-century French psychiatrist.

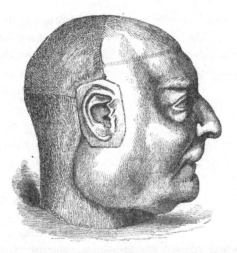

William R. Wilde

The plaster mask taken of Dean Swift, from which a bust was made.

inclined to believe, the best likeness of Swift – during, at least, the last few years of his life – now in existence.

"In the Museum of Trinity College, Dublin, there is a dark plaster bust, or cast, of Dean Swift. It is an impression taken from the mask applied to the face after death. The expression of countenance is most unequivocally maniacal, and one side of the mouth (the left) horribly contorted downwards, as if convulsed by pain."

That his not speaking was not the result either of insanity or imbecility, but arose either from paralysis of the muscles by which the mechanism of speech is produced or from loss of memory of the things which he wished to express, as frequently occurs in cases of cerebral disease, cannot be doubted.

The disease under which he laboured so long we have ventured to term cerebral congestion. For the last few years of his embittered existence – from his seventy-fifth to his seventy-eighth year – his disease partook so much of the nature of senile decay or the dementia of old age, that it is difficult, with the materials now at command, to define by any precise medical term his actual state.

It is related by one of Swift's most recent biographers, that Richard Brennan, to whom we have already referred, "the servant in whose arms he died, stated that one of the few instances of a lucid interval during his fatal malady was a glimmering consciousness of his birth day, which he showed by frequently repeating, when it came round, 'let the day perish wherein I was born and the night in which it was said there was a man child conceived'."

It is difficult to eradicate long-cherished opinions. It is hard to persuade

the great mass of the people, in this city at least, that the Dean was not one
of the first, if not the very first inmate of his own madhouse, although that
building was not erected until many years after his death. With the educated
and the learned these unworthy lines –

"From Marlb'rough's eyes the streams of dotage flow,
And Swift expires a driv'ler and a show."

– pass current, not for mere imbecility and second childishness, but for
absolute insanity; and it is no easy task to uproot this idea.

The Closing Years of Dean Swift's Life with Remarks on Stella
Dr. William R. Wilde, M.R.I.A., F.R.C.S.
1849

THE
DEATHS

There is no newspaper in Ireland in which the first page is the first to be read. It is customary, through a constitutional compulsion, to skip to The Deaths. For the dead are more important to us than the living: they say less, but mean more. And the Irish have always managed to squeeze more entertainment from a funeral than a wedding.

'Happy is the bride that the sun shines on;
But blessed is the corpse that the rain rains on.'

A proverb

DIED IN THE PULPIT

Rev. Lindsay H. Cullen, superintendent minister of the Dublin Central Mission of the Methodist Church, died suddenly recently whilst conducting a service in the School Chapel of Wesley College, St. Stephen's Green, Dublin. Mr. Cullen, who had conducted the morning service, left home, apparently, in the best of health, to conduct the special school service for the pupils of Wesley College. He had just led the congregation in the repetition of the Lord's Prayer when he slipped down at the desk. Quickly, he was carried into the vestry, when it was seen that life was extinct.

Daily Telegraph
November 17th, 1930

DEATH OF A BISHOP AND HIS WIFE

Dublin: Right Rev. Frederick R. Wynne, D.D., Episcopal Bishop of Killaloe, Kilfenora and Clonfert, was found dead at 5:30 this morning on the sidewalk near his residence in this city. The wife of the Bishop of Killaloe was found dead, in her bedroom, soon after the body of the Bishop was discovered on the sidewalk. An investigation of the strange death of the Bishop of Killaloe and his wife shows that the prelate recently left Killaloe for his home in Dublin, on account of his wife's health, and had left the house to fetch a doctor for her at about 5:30a.m., when he fell dead near his residence. His wife must have died soon after the Bishop left the house. [I have to ask: where were the servants?]

Spencer Herald, New York
January 5th, 1907

ACT OF HEROISM CUT TRAGICALLY SHORT

A Malahide railway porter named Henry Cooney met with fatal injuries in removing from the line an obstacle which threatened to wreck a train. Cooney, standing on Malahide platform, as a passenger train came into the station, saw a large trunk fall down between the rails. He jumped immediately from the platform and removed the trunk just in time. But he did so at the cost of his own life for he was struck by the engine and dashed against the line, receiving a fracture of the skull. The unfortunate man was conveyed under medical care to Amiens Street Station and thence to Jervis Street Hospital. He died, however, in the course of the afternoon. Cooney, who was about forty years of age, averted by his self-sacrifice what might have been a serious accident to the train.

The *Witness*
July 3rd, 1914

SHOCKING OCCURRENCE IN DUBLIN

Yesterday morning, shortly after one o'clock, a fatal accident occurred under strange circumstances in Dublin. It appears that, at the hour mentioned, a man named James Dobbin, 30 Werburgh Street, while sitting in the front drawing-room of the house, told his wife that he wished to go out to get a drink. She remonstrated with him and eventually refused to allow him to leave the house. Dobbin then stated that if he were not allowed to go out by the hall door he would find another mode of exit. He then went to the front window, raised it, and partially lifted himself out upon the window sill. Having remained in this position for a few moments, he made an effort to draw himself back, but in doing so lost his balance and fell into the street, a distance of about 16 feet. The unfortunate man alighted on his head and sustained a fracture of the skull, death being almost instantaneous.

Belfast Evening Telegraph
August 19th, 1895

DEATH BY POISON

On Monday morning, an industrious female, named Byrne, who resides at Blackrock, being very thirsty, drank off a quantity of a mineral preparation, which she had been using to clean straw bonnets, mistaking it for water; she returned to her bed, when, after the lapse of ten minutes, she discovered the mistake. The stomach-pump was used, but had no effect. The unfortunate girl died the same day.

Belfast Newsletter
July 9th, 1833

DEATHS

Tuesday night a Stonecutter [MR. SHEEHAN] in Marlborough-street being in a violent fever, got out of bed and jumped out of the window two stories high, but received little hurt, went as far as the Old-bridge, where he was stopped by the watchman and brought home, but died two hours after.

Pue's Occurrences or Impartial Occurrence
July 14th, 1741

Last Tuesday, Mr. [THOMAS] Sutton, Goldsmith on Cork-hill, having rode into the watering place on the gravel walk, to let his horse drink, was thrown off by his horse plunging into a deep place and was drowned.

Dublin Chronicle
April 30th, 1745

Monday morning died MR. ROWE, an eminent Painter in Aungier-street. He went to bed, seemingly in perfect Health, but started suddenly out of his sleep, stuck by his wife with his elbow, who cried out, you have killed me. Mr. Rowe, instantly answered, I am dead by myself, and expired immediately.

Dublin Chronicle
November 30th, 1750

On Thursday last, PETER BROWN a Stucco-plasterer was drinking a dram with some friends; in swallowing the liquor, his breath was stopped and he instantly died.

Dublin Chronicle
February 15th, 1752

Mr. [Richard] CARVER, senior painter, finding himself suddenly taken ill as he was walking on College-green, entered into a house and instantly expired.

Dublin Courier
February 12th, 1754

At his lodgings on College-green, aged 96, SIGNIOR FRANCISCEO GEMINIANI, well-known by the lovers of harmony.

Dublin Courant
September 17th, 1762

MYSTERIOUS DEATH

On Tuesday evening, a publican, of the name of Denis Mullowney, residing in Clare-lane, reported to the Magistrates of College-street, that a man, named O'Hara, who had formerly been servant to Mr. Blennerhasset, of Mount-street, had locked himself in a room, in his (Mullowney's) house, since the Sunday preceding, and no person could obtain admission to the apartment. Peace Officers Montgomery and Needham were accordingly sent to Mullowney's house and, receiving no answer on their demanding admittance to the room, they forced upon the door, when they discovered the body of O'Hara lying dead on the floor, without any marks of violence on his person. The City Coroner was yesterday made acquainted with the circumstance, but, with the usual discrimination by which the coroners of this country are distinguished, he did not consider it a case that required the holding of an inquest.

Freeman's Journal
February 8th, 1827

MELANCHOLY SUICIDE

On Tuesday night last, between eight and nine o'clock, Oliver Moore, Esq. of Dublin, shot himself with a pistol, in a field behind Marina-terrace, in the immediate vicinity of this town*. The ball entered his right temple, which, of course, caused instant death. The unfortunate gentleman had been labouring for some time past under mental depression and was recommended to the island for change of air, by his physician, where he arrived a few weeks since.

The Tablet
March 2nd, 1844

DISSUASIVE AGAINST SUICIDE

Suggested by the melancholy influence of the unfortunate Chaplain to the Tower of London, which appeared in the papers:-

If you are distressed in mind, live; serenity and joy may yet dawn upon your soul.

If you have been contented and cheerful, live; and generously diffuse that happiness to others.

---

* The town was Douglas, as Mr. Moore was recuperating on the Isle of Man.

If misfortunes have befallen you by your own misconduct, live; and be wiser for the future.

If they have befallen you by the faults of others, live; you have nothing wherewith to reproach yourself.

If you are indignant and helpless, live; the face of things may agreeably change.

If you are rich and prosperous, live; and enjoy what you possess.

If another hath injured you, live; his own crime will be his punishment.

If you have injured another, live; and recompense him by your good offices.

If your character be attacked unjustly, live; time will remove the aspersion.

If the reproaches are well-founded, live; and deserve them not for the future.

If you are already eminent and applauded, live; and preserve the honours you have acquired.

If you have been negligent and useless to society, live; and make amends by your future conduct.

If you have been active and industrious, live; and communicate your improvements to others.

If you have been wise and virtuous, live; for the future benefit of mankind. And lastly:

If you hope for immortality, live; and prepare to enjoy it.

Freeman's Journal
November 6th, 1804

THE CHAPEL FOXES

On October 28, 1907, Jenico Preston, the 14th Viscount [Gormanston], died in Dublin. About 8 o'clock that night, the coachman and gardener saw two foxes near the chapel (close to the house), five or six more round the front of the house and several crying in the "cloisters." Two days later, the Hon. Richard Preston, R.F.A., was watching by his father's body in the above chapel. About 3 A.M., he became conscious of a slight noise, which seemed to be that of a number of people walking stealthily around the chapel on the gravel walk. He went to the side door, listened, and heard outside a continuous and insistent snuffling or sniffing noise, accompanied by whimperings and scratchings at the door. On opening it, he saw a full-grown fox sitting on the path within four feet of him. Just in the shadow was another, while he could hear several more moving close by in the darkness. He then went to the end door, opposite the altar, and, on opening it, saw two more foxes, one so close that he could have touched it with his foot. On shutting the door, the noise continued till 5 A.M., when it suddenly ceased[*].

New Ireland Review
April 1908

Illustrated Police News

A GRAVESIDE DISTURBANCE

Our first story, which is sent us by Mr. De Lacy of Dublin, deals with an incident that occurred in the early part of the last century. An epidemic which was then rife in the city was each day taking its toll on the unhappy citizens. The wife of a man living in Merrion Square was stricken down and hastily buried in a churchyard in Donnybrook which is now closed. On the night after the funeral, one of the city police, or "Charlies" as they were

---

[*] Indeed, the family foxes were known to wake the passing of each master of Gormanston Castle, Co. Meath, beginning at least as early as 1786 with the 11th Viscount. However, the death in Dublin of the 14th Viscount was the first to prove that distance was no barrier to the animals' psychical reach.

then called, passed through the churchyard on his rounds. When nearing the centre, he was alarmed to hear a sound coming from a grave close at hand and, turning, saw a white apparition sit up and address him. This was all he waited for; with a shriek, he dropped his lantern and staff and made off as fast as his legs would carry him. The apparition thereupon took up the lamp and staff and walked to Merrion Square to the house of mourning, was admitted by the servants, and, to the joy of the whole household, was found to be the object of their grief returned, Alcestis-like* , from the grave. It seems that the epidemic was so bad that the bodies of the victims were interred hastily and without much care: the unfortunate lady had really been in a state of coma or trance and, as the grave was lightly covered, when she came to she was able to force her way up and seeing the "Charlie" passing, she called for assistance.

True Irish Ghost Stories
St. John D. Seymour and Harry L. Neligan
1914

THE REVERIE

The other dream, which occurred only last year, was to this effect: I was riding outside an omnibus in London when a bat suddenly flew past me. All my fellow-passengers cried out in a chorus, 'How remarkable! A bat!' and I awoke actually repeating those words. I was so impressed that I jotted down the dream in my memorandum book.

Exactly a week later, I received tidings of my father's death: he had been thrown from a trap, whilst descending a steep hill near Dublin, and killed on the spot.

Meaning of Dreams
Elliott O'Donnell
1911

Yesterday morning, the remains of the late Alderman Poole was interred in the Cabbage-garden. The funeral was very respectably attended; the most of the Board of Aldermen were present and a considerable number of other eminent Citizens.

Freeman's Journal
March 1st, 1804

---

* Alcestis was the wife of King Admetus and, like so many spouses of Greek mythology, was rescued from the afterlife because eternity did not suit her heartbroken husband. In this case, Heracles saved her as a thank-you gift to Admetus for his hospitality.

INTERMENT BY NIGHT

Burial at night was … quite the customary thing. Richard Helsham, a celebrated Dublin physician, gave directions in his will, made in 1738, that he was to be buried at night, with only one attendant, bearing a taper, to be present. Miss Griselda Steevens too, in her will made in 1740, directed that she should be buried late at night in St. Peter's Church. In point of fact, she was buried in Steeven's Hospital and, not once only, but three times. Dr. Kirkpatrick suggests that it was customary to exhume and rebury a coffin after the lapse of a week and he proffers a rather unsavoury theory for this practice, though quite possibly it was to make sure that the body-snatchers had not been at work. In the case of "Madame Steevens," the third interment took place when her remains were removed for burial in the Hospital Chapel.

Dublin Historical Record
June–August 1948

SKIRMISH AT THE CEMETERY

In 1853, the bloodhounds which had so long guarded Glasnevin Cemetery bayed no more. How the Committee came to relinquish the services of those vigilant and faithful creatures arose in this way. An annual stipend had been paid to a physician to attend, in case of illness, the Cemetery staff.

Samara Leibner

Dr. Kirwan, the well-known City Coroner, was the last to fill this post. One night, when hurrying through the Cemetery to visit Mr. Walker, the sexton, Dr. Kirwan was suddenly attacked by the bloodhounds. Their mission from the first had been one of hostility to such medical men as dared to invade the Cemetery at night; and, with canine instinct, they are said to have scented on this occasion a son of Galen. Dr. Kirwan, placing his back against a tombstone, sought to keep the blood hounds at bay and, for some minutes, the City Coroner was in imminent risk of furnishing in his own person a sensational case for inquest on the morrow. At last his lusty cries for help were heard above the canine chorus. Help arrived and, thus, Dr. Kirwan narrowly escaped the fate of Actaeon[*]. The nocturnal incident naturally caused a shock[**]. As a result, the bloodhounds were banished. But, in point of fact, the outrages which they had been got to prevent had long previously ceased, thanks to the operation of the Anatomy Act.

History of the Cemeteries of Dublin
William Fitzpatrick
1900

---

[*] Having been transformed into a stag by Artemis, for misconduct against the goddess, he was ripped apart by his own hounds.

[**] Dr. Kirwan was attacked near the Old Chapel Circle and close to the spot where his own tomb now stands. It records that his death took place on 3rd February, 1868.

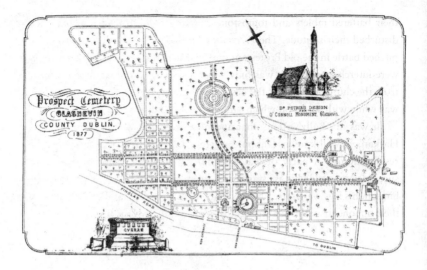

RAISING DEAD BODIES

Between two and three o'clock yesterday morning, the guard of the 26th Foot on duty at Kilmainham, from some suspicious appearances, were led to examine a gentleman's gig, which was stopping on the road opposite the Hospital-fields, better known by the name of Bully's Acre. Their suspicions turned out to be well-founded, for, in the gig, were several dead bodies closely packed, which had been just disintered. The gig and two men who were in charge of it were sent to Arran-quay Police-office by the guard. Mr. Cooper, Chief-constable, caused the bodies to be re-intered; the gig, and the men, who gave their names as James Fitzgallon and John Byrne, have been detained, until the circumstances can be fully investigated.

Freeman's Journal
February 8th, 1827

It had long been a practice with the medical profession to visit graveyards at night, in order to exhume bodies for anatomical dissection. Indeed, there was practically no other way, except by theft, to attain their scientific object. Frequent and, at times, sanguinary collisions took place between the "Sack-em-ups" and the "Dead Watchers", in one of which the son of Dr. Kirby, President of the College of Surgeons, was shot dead. The rural graveyards of Kilgobbin, Killester, and Churchtown present to this day, in their battered tablets and tombstones, traces of the fusillades which once disturbed their solitude. The *Freeman's Journal*, of 1830, records a regular pitched battle in the old Protestant graveyard at Glasnevin. A hundred shots were interchanged and it was only when a watcher rang out an alarm peal from the church tower that the besiegers decamped. The ground, it is added, was white with snow, on which "might be traced drops of blood."

It was in "Bully's Acre" that an untoward calamity had befallen Peter Harkan, a well-known Dublin surgeon, and hitherto a very successful resurrectionist. A party of watchers having suddenly rushed forward, he succeeded in getting his assistants over the cemetery wall, but, when crossing himself, his legs were seized by the watchmen, while his pupils pulled against their opponents with such strength that he eventually died from the effects.

History of the Cemeteries of Dublin
William Fitzpatrick
1900

RESURRECTIONS

On Monday a highly respectable lady, Mrs. E. Nicholson, was summoned before the magistrates at the Head Office, by Mr. Wharton, churchwarden of Peter's parish, for having committed a trespass in the churchyard, by having deposited there a coffin filled with sticks and stones. Mrs. Nicholson, in her defence, stated that she had paid for the ground in which the coffin was interred and that she resorted to this strategem to save the body of her son from

the clutch of the resurrectionists. She produced a certificate of the clergyman in a distant part of Ireland, where the body had been really interred. In seeking for the body, the resurrectionists discovered the trick that had been played on them. Under these circumstances, the proceeding against Mrs. Nicholson was abandoned.

Freeman's Journal
February 29th, 1832

THE BODIES IN ST. MICHAN'S

A learned chemist in this city published an article in a periodical paper, on the appearance of the remains deposited in these vaults, from which the following is a brief abstract:

Now the floor, walls, and atmosphere of the vaults are perfectly dry and the walls are composed of a stone peculiarly calculated to resist moisture. Further, it appears that in none of the bodies deposited here are any intestines

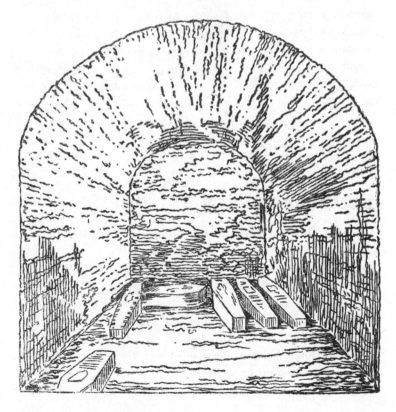

or other parts containing fluid matter to be found, having all decayed shortly after burial. In one vault is shown the remains of a nun, who died at the advanced age of 111; the body has now been 30 years in this mansion of death and, although there is scarcely a remnant of the coffin, is as completely preserved, with the exception of the hair, as if it had been embalmed. In the same vault are to be seen the bodies of two Roman Catholic clergymen, which have been 50 years deposited here, even more perfect than the nun. In general, it was evident that the old were much better preserved than the young.

The Picture of Dublin: or, Stranger's Guide to the Irish Metropolis
William Curry
1835

EXTRAORDINARY STORY IN DUBLIN COURTS

An extraordinary story was told in Dublin Criminal Court yesterday, when Patrick Connor was sentenced to 12 months' imprisonment, with hard labour, for neglecting to provide Christian or decent burial for his mother in February, 1924, at Oughterard, Connemara.

Counsel for the State said the original charge was one of murder, but it was reduced to the horrible one of burying his mother as if she were a brute. The woman disappeared for five months and it shed an extraordinary light on the conditions prevailing in the country at the time that not one of her neighbours said a word about her disappearance. When asked where his mother was, accused gave

various excuses, the last one being that she had gone to America.
The police began to dig the garden and came upon the remains of
Mrs Connor, accused having first told them – "Don't dig there.
You will get the remains of a pig in it that my father buried." The
State did not indict him for murder, because the doctors could not
prove from the decomposed remains that the woman had met with a
violent death. In a bag in the house, the police found 23 sovereigns.

In sentencing prisoner, the Judge said the fact that such a thing
could happen was a disgrace to the community of which they all
formed part.

Glasgow Herald
June 17th, 1925

STATEMENT OF MAGISTRATE
MR. C.J. O'DONEL,

On the accusation that staff of Cemetery of Propsect, Glasnevin
had, contrary to public decency, disinterred several bodies and
human remains, while in the ordinary course of their duties.

"Now, is it not within the knowledge of every man who has buried a
relation in a grave, that the gravediggers come upon thigh-bones, rib-bones,
and skulls? And are not these bones and skulls the remains of his own
deceased ancestors or relatives? And, if he follows the coffin, does he not
see those bones piled on the freshly-lifted clay, waiting for the coffin to be
put back in its place? Is not that our every-day experience? For my part, it
has been my sad duty to witness it on a great many occasions and, on those
occasions, I saw the bones that were left on the side of the grave put back
into the grave before it was refilled. It is untenable to say that it is an act of
desecration to put clean bones on the side of a grave. If it is, it is an act of
desecration that is committed by members of every family. And I say that,
if it is not an act of desecration, for the head of a family to do this, it is not
an act of desecration if it is done by the trustees of this Cemetery.

"I say it is a monstrous thing that, without a shadow of ground for
sustaining this charge, the process of this court should be prostituted for
the purpose of private malignity. It is a monstrous thing that citizens of
the highest position in this city should have such a charge brought against
them, and without the slightest shadow of foundation for the proceeding."

1870

ST. PATRICK'S CATHEDRAL

In a press in the Chapter-house a skull, said to be that of Duke Schomberg, is still preserved, in the forehead of which is a circular aperture made by the bullet which caused his death.

The Picture of Dublin: or, Stranger's Guide to the Irish Metropolis
William Curry
1835

ON THE DISCOVERY OF THREE EARTHEN VASES AT PALMERSTOWN

Portions of three earthen vases were recently obtained at Palmerstown, county of Dublin, all of which unfortunately broken into pieces by the rude treatment they got when found by the labourers. One of these urns, of small size, presents little of interest. The second, in which human bones were discovered, was of unusual bulk, its mouth measuring eleven inches in diameter; its peculiar style of ornamentation is also deserving of remark. Around the third vase, the mouth of which was about seven inches in diameter, was built a carefully constructed kist of flags; it contained portions of the bones of a human being, two fragments of shell, and also some dog bones; a strange assemblage that remind us of the "Kitchen Middens" of Denmark and of our own shores, in which human remains are found mixed with shells and, occasionally, also the bones of man's faithful companion in the chase, his dog.

Proceedings of the Royal Irish Academy,
Volume 10, 1836–1869

STRANGE DISCOVERY

Yesterday, while a labourer in the employment of Mr. Manifold of 22, Richmond-hill, Rathmines, was engaged digging in a garden at the rear of the house, he turned up a human skull and, on digging further, found a number of small human bones. These bones were perfectly dry and must have been lying where they were discovered for many years. An inquiry will be made into the circumstances this day.

Freeman's Journal
March 6th, 1860

BONE MANURE

Bone manure (drilled 25 bushels to the acre) is the best and cheapest for turnips, (six quarters per acre, sown broad cast) for wheat and barley, if the farmer can procure the latter at 5s per quarter. The only positive rule as to the certainty of bones acting as a manure on untried land is to notice any that may have been spread on the ground by accident. If they continue white without moss attaching to them, as is the case on cold clay and some other soils, there they will not act as a manure; but if, on the contrary, they soon become brown and mossy, there they will act as a powerful manure.

Freeman's Journal
February 29th, 1832

MARRIAGES BILL
LIST OF MINISTERS
Of the Protestant Church of Ireland,
IN THE CITY OF DUBLIN
WHO HAVE PETITIONED PARLIAMENT
IN FAVOUR OF THE BILL FOR
Legalising Marriage with a Deceased Wife's Sister.

The following Ministers of the Protestant Church of Ireland, in the City of Dublin, have petitioned both Houses of Parliament on different occasions in favour of the Bill for Legalising Marriage with a Deceased Wife's Sister:

The Rev. Hercules Dickenson, D.D., Vicar of St. Anne's, Dean, Chaplain to the Lord Lieutenant.
The Rev. Charles M. Fleury, D.D., Chaplain Molyneux Asylum.
The Rev. Maurice Neglian, D.D., Chaplain Molyneux Asylum.
The Rev. R.T. Smith, M.A., Chaplain St. Stephen's.
The Rev. James Andrew, Curate St. Michael's.
The Rev. John Black, M.A., Curate St. Mary's.
The Rev. F. Carmichael, M.A., Chaplain Magdalen Asylum, Chaplain to the Lord Lieutenant.
The Rev. William G. Carroll, M.A., Vicar St. Bride's.
The Rev. E.A. Carroll, M.A., Curate Trinity Church.
The Rev. James Carson, M.A., Curate St. Mary's.
The Rev. William Marrable, D.D., Rector St. Andrew's.
The Rev. Thomas Long, M.A., Curate St. John's.
The Rev. J.F. Lucas, D.D., Curate St. Philip's, Chaplain to the Lord Lieutenant.
The Rev. Charles E. Tisdall, D.D., Chancellor Christ Church, and Rector St. Dolough's.
The Rev. W.T.H. Le Fanu, Rector St. Paul's and Chaplain to the Lord Lieutenant.

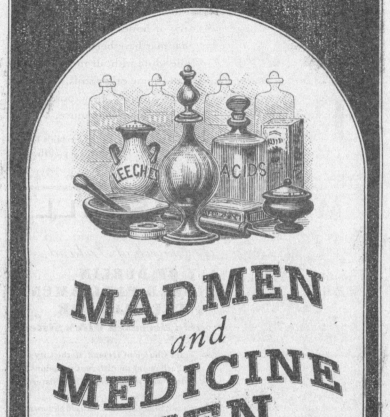

MADMEN
and
MEDICINE
MEN

The first hospital in Ireland was Jervis Street — the Charitable Infirmary — founded by six benevolent surgeons in 1718. Of course, it was first on Cook Street, then on King's Inn Quay. It is now a shopping centre. By trial, error, and assimilation, medicine is always progressing. Mercer's Hospital, founded in 1734, is, mercifully, a medical centre. Dr. Steeven's Hospital of 1733, which, as we know, housed a pig-faced lady, is now a Health Executive administrative centre. The number of pig-faced people inside has probably changed. Everything changes. Except for chronic conditions, for which there is always Hydriodate of Potash; Iodides of Mercury; Æthers, Sulphuric and Nitric; Hyrdrocyanic of Prussic Acid; phrenology; bloodletting; and wishful thinking.

NOTE FROM A MEDICAL PROFESSIONAL

Envy has ever been the predominant passion of pretenders to art and science. Whenever a person, eminent in his profession, makes his appearance, an outcry is immediately raised against him by the most ignorant and, consequently, the greatest imposers on the public. This I have sufficiently experienced since my arrival in this Kingdom. I am a Surgeon, regularly bred in Paris, and have practised in this City for two years, with remarkable success, though to the great offence of my brethren who, for no other reason but because I perform cures in half the time, quarter of the expense, and without wasting my patients after a tedious course of ill-judged medicines, industriously made out that my method of proceeding is inconsistent with regular practice, and the French know nothing of surgery, etc. Notwithstanding the opposition of such, I intend to settle in this City and hope to demonstrate by my skill and assiduity that all imputations to the prejudice of the character are equally groundless and malicious.

Universal Advertiser
1754

AN ACT OF MEDICAL DETECTIVE WORK

It is not unworthy the relating an experiment of my own of this kind, about the year 1660. I being upon practice in Dublin, there came to my House there, a rich Citizen on the behalf of his Wife, who had lain sick about two Months and had made use of most of the Eminent Doctors in Town; but, having no remedy, he desired my assistance and visit; when I saw her in great agony by an inflammation and burning she complained of in her Belly and Womb, which she and the standers-by said came to her in fits. I enquired of her Self, Husband and Friends, what might be the first cause, which they all being ignorant of, they told me she was bewitched, for the violent Fits came so exactly in time, Mornings and Evenings. I read Sir K. Digby and some other Books of Sympathy and Antipathy, which did the more fasten it in my mind, that some strange trick or magick art had been used upon her. Her Husband being a Soap-Boiler by Trade, it came into my mind to ask the Maid Servant and made her shew me where she emptied her Mistress's Pots of Water, so I went with her where was a great heap of Ashes made in Soap-Boiling, this standing nearer to her by much than the necessary House, she usually threw her Water upon the Ashes to save her labour of going further; after I saw this cause of her Mistress's Disease, I told her she was the Witch that had bewitched her Mistress, and forbade her for the future to empty any more there and, having found the cause, declared it to them, but advised the sick Woman for some time after, constantly to Urine in a Basin half-full of fair Water, by which only means she was by God's Blessing perfectly and presently Cured, to their great Joy, and my good Reward.

Secrets Disclosed of Consumptions Shewing How to Distinguish between Scurvy and Venereal Disease; also, How to Prevent and Cure the Fistula by Chymical Drops without Cutting; also Piles, Hæmorrhoids, and other Diseases
John Archer
1684

A SELECTION OF MEDICAL AND ZOOLOGICAL PRESENTATIONS GIVEN BY THE DUBLIN PHILOSOPHICAL SOCIETY IN ITS FIRST FOUR YEARS (1683–1687)

Dr. Allen Moulin — Experiments on the Blood; On Poisons; Dissection of a Man who died of Consumption; On the Peculiarities of the Pulse; On Ovarian Disease; Experiments, consisting of injecting Fluids into the Thorax of Animals; On the Organs of Respiration and Circulation, by removing a Portion of a Dog's Lung, &c. — Dissection of a Monstrous Kitten; and a Chicken with two Bills; On Ligature of the Jugular Vein in a Dog.

Mr. R. Buckley — On the Dissection of a Bat.

Mr. St. George Ashe. — On a remarkable Case of Haemorrhage; On Hermaphrodism; Account of a Man in Galway who suckled his Child and had Pendulous Mammae.

Mr. R. Bulkeley. — Experiments on venous and arterial Blood; Discourse on Mr. Boyle's Book on Human Blood.

Dr. Willoughby. — On Hermaphrodism.

Dr. Huoglaghan. — Description of a Human Kidney weighing forty-two Ounces; On the Dissection of a Monstrous Child with two Heads and three Arms.*

---

* "Dr. Huoglaghan informed the S. that having dissected the Child with 2 heads, 3 arms &c. mentioned formerly, he found that all the inward parts were double except the liver (which was as big as 2 livers) & the heart not much above the ordinary dimension." Minutes of the Dublin Philosophical Society, June 22nd, 1685.

ON THE ANATOMY OF THE ELEPHANT

One of the earliest dissections of the elephant on record is that which was made in Dublin, in 1682, by A. Moulin, a medical graduate of Trinity College. This animal was destroyed by a fire which accidentally occurred in the city.

Robert Harrison
Proceedings of the Royal Irish Academy
Vol.3, 1844–1847

THE FIRST DISSECTION IN IRELAND

Dissection was, it appears, but very rarely performed in Dublin at this time.

"About a fortnight ago, Dr. Dunn procured the body of a malefactor to dissect and make a skeleton of. I was constant at the dissection, but nothing curious was done, but only the chirurgeons and physicians that were present spoke at random, as the parts presented themselves; it lasted for a week."

Dublin University Magazine
Vol. 18, 1841

A SURGEON'S STORY

Some three or four years since, a friend of mine, whom I shall call Ormsby removed from his chambers in the University and entered himself as a resident medical student in Steevens's Hospital, Dublin.

The day on which the incident I am going to relate occurred, a brother student had dined with him in his rooms and the cloth had only been removed when a porter entered and told Ormsby in a whisper that the patient in the fever ward had just died. "Very well, bring him to the dead room. Drury, you will wait, I'll shew you a beautiful operation."

"No, I thank you, I have got quite enough of the work today; I have attended a demonstration – chemical lecture – remained six hours in Park-street and Egad! I'll have no more of it. It is now after six o'clock and I must be off. Bon soir."

"Thoughtless fellow!" said Ormsby, as he took up his candle and proceeded to the dissecting room. To an uninitiated stranger it would have appeared a horrible and ghastly sight; gentle reader, I shall not describe it,

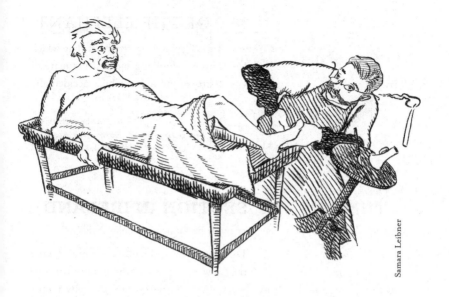

Samara Leibner

yet so much are we the slaves of habit that the young surgeon sat down to his revolting tasks as indifferently as, reader, you would open your chess board. The room was lofty and extensive, badly lighted; his flickering taper scarcely revealing the ancient writings that he was about to peruse. On the table before him lay the subject, wrapped in a long sheet, his case of instruments resting on it, he read on for some time intently, unheeding the storm which raged without, and threatened to blow in the casements against which the rain beat in large drops; and this, said he, looking on the body and pursuing the train of his thoughts, this mass of lifelessness, coldness, and inaction, is all we know of that alteration of our being, that mysterious modification of our existence by which our vital intelligence is launched into the worlds beyond... a breath and we are here... a breath and we are gone. He raised his knife and opened a vein in the foot. A faint shriek and a start, which overset the table and extinguished the light were the effects of his temerity. Though somewhat shocked, Ormsby was not daunted and then turned to relight his taper, he heard through the darkness a long-drawn sigh and in weak and sickly accents – "Oh! Doctor, I am a great deal better now." Ormsby said nothing, but returning deliberately, covered up the man thus wonderfully re-awakened from an almost fatal trance, carried him back, and laid him in his bed. A week after the patient was discharged from the hospital cured.

Dublin Penny Journal
January 25th, 1834

SINGULARLY USEFUL PROPERTIES OF GARLIC

The smell of garlic, which is formidable to many ladies is, perhaps, the most infallible remedy in the world against the vapours and the nervous disorders to which women are subject.

Dublin Penny Journal
September 14th, 1833

HAIR TURNING SUDDENLY GREY

A young and comely married lady in Dublin, remarkable for the beauty of her hair, was accustomed to drive in her jaunting-car with some of her family every day during the summer, to Clontarf, to bathe. On one occasion, her horse, a very spirited animal, took fright and ran furiously along the strand road. She clung to the rails and in this way was hurried along in the highest state of terror and excitement. At length the wheel came in contact with a rock which projected from the side of the road and the car and horse were both upturned. When the people came to her relief, she was discovered under the car in a state of insensibility. A violent fever supervened and her medical attendants thought it necessary to have her hair cut off. The barber who attended me was the person sent for. He had often cut and dressed her hair before and he anticipated, in the way of his business, the beautiful and valuable tresses he was likely to obtain on the occasion. He, next day, complained to me of his disappointment. He could not recognise that which he had so much admired a few weeks before – it was quite grey; the specimen he showed me as a curiosity was like that of a woman of seventy years old.

Dublin Penny Journal
January 30th, 1836

PHRENOLOGY

M r Alexander Wilson of Dublin opposes the common opinion "that the Irish have larger Combativeness than the Scotch" and says he is fully satisfied, from his observations in Ireland during the last eighteen months, that the genuine Irish have only a moderate endowment of that organ; much less than is found in the Scotch or their descendants in the north of Ireland. "Although often rash in their conduct, their rashness does not proceed from deficient Cautiousness, the organ of fear; but from excited Destructiveness,

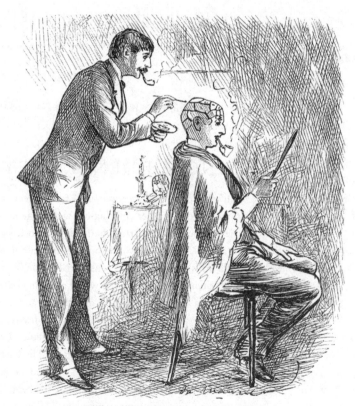

NEW IDEA FOR A FANCY BALL.
Shave your Head, and go as a Phrenological Bust.

the propensity to injure, and inability to perceive consequences, resulting from deficient Causality."

Phrenological Journal and Magazine of Moral Science
Vol. 16, 1843

SIZE OF HEAD, NATIONAL AND PROVINCIAL

R especting the Irish head, it is stated in the second volume of the *Phrenological Journal*, page 17, that the heads of the educated classes in Dublin are generally small; and information is required by the writer from some London hatter as to the average size of fine hats sent to that city, anticipating that they are inferior in sizes to those sold in London and Edinburgh. In so far as I know, I am not enabled to confirm this statement, as the average sizes of fine hats sent from this city to Dublin are superior to those in the London trade. The general request is to send a large and not small sizes, the latter remaining useless upon the shelves; the scales always observed is above the London average and orders are sometimes received equal in size to the full Scotch head.

NOTE: There is a great population in Dublin and within the Pale, as it was called, essentially English; still the prevalence of moderate-sized heads was there observed in the better classes. In the theatre or at an assembly, in Dublin, for example, the heads of the men appeared to the eye to be smaller than the heads of the same classes in London or Edinburgh. Of the lower Irish heads, the author does not speak. – EDITOR

Phrenological Journal and Science of Health
Vol. 2, 1840

REPORT OF MR COMBE'S VISIT TO DUBLIN

Sir, at the request of the Council of the Phrenological Society, I read to an extraordinary meeting of the Society, held on 14th May, a Report of several Phrenological Observations made during my late visit to Dublin.

I am, &c.

Geo. Combe.

1. Case of Bridget Smith

MERCER'S HOSPITAL, DUBLIN, 15TH APRIL, 1829

Present – Surgeon Auchinleck and about twenty medical students.

A woman was presented to Mr Combe as a convalescent patient and he was requested to examine her head and say if there was anything remarkable in the development of the organs. Mr. Combe requested one of the young gentlemen to write down the development, which he dictated.

The gentlemen present then retired with Mr Combe to another apartment, when Mr Combe remarked that he understood the woman was not insane (Mr. Auchinleck said she was not). Mr. Combe added, "It is impossible to speak of actions; all that I can do is to indicate dispositions or tendencies."

Mr. Auchinleck asked **what combination gives the tendency to suicide? Mr Combe answered that, in his System of Phrenology, under the head of Cautiousness, it is stated, that "Dr. A. Combe examined a considerable number of suicides in the morgue at Paris and found in them Hope generally small, with Cautiousness and Destructiveness large."**

Her history was well known in the ward, that she had been married seven years, had no children, that her husband had not lived with her for fifteen months; and that jealousy was the cause of her attempt at suicide both times. She herself stated that "she wished to die before her husband's eyes and that she loves the very ground he walks on."

2. Case of Mr Oldham

On 15th April, 1829, Mr Combe was taken by Mr Carr, one of the directors of the Bank of Ireland, to see that establishment. In one of the apartments Mr Carr presented to Mr Combe a respectable looking gentleman, above the middle period of life, telling him that he was an extraordinary character and requesting him to say for what qualities he was distinguished. Mr Combe had not the slightest idea who the gentleman was. After examining the head, he dictated the following remarks:

"The head indicates a general capacity for painting and the imitative arts and, in general, the mind, if turned to mechanics or any other similar pursuit is so constituted as to excel."

Mr Carr then mentioned that the gentleman's name was Mr Oldham and proceeded to show Mr Combe his work. He was taken to a separate building, where a steam-engine was in motion, which had been constructed from Mr Oldham's drawings and projections. Upstairs he found the engine printing bank-notes and registering the paper given out and the printed notes returned. This machinery was contrived and executed by Mr Oldham. Mr Oldham also showed Mr Combe two very pretty profiles in watercolours, painted by himself, and told him that he had constructed an organ with a vox humana pipe, which delivers syllables in a manner resembling human articulation. Finally, Mr Oldham described all these things with a fluency which, as Mr Combe remarked afterwards, manifested a great organ of language.

PEMPHIGUS GANGRENOSIS OF THE AURICLE.

This disease was first described by Dr. Whitely Stokes and mentioned by Dr. Wilde in the medical memoir attached to the census of Ireland in 1841. It is peculiar to Ireland, very apt to attack children on or about the ears, is very fatal, and prevails especially among the lower orders. It is said to have caused 17,799 deaths in ten years in Ireland, the truth of which, Wilde is inclined to believe. It is not known in this country, though the scars left by it have been seen by the author, in an Irish woman.

Gangrene of the ears occurs in some low fevers; it may be symmetrical and associated with gangrene of the nose. It is usually a very bad symptom, being the immediate precursor of death in most cases. It is generally associated with livid and gangrenous spots elsewhere on the body.

The Ear
C.H. Burnett
1884

ON BLOODLETTING

It is obvious that no specific rule for regulating the quantity of blood to be drawn can be established: this matter must always be left to the discretion of the practitioner. It is my duty, however, more especially as I have the name of being an advocate for bloodletting in fevers, to state, that several cases have come to my knowledge in which full bloodletting, practised when the disease was confirmed, proved injurious: great prostration followed; and, although the local determination, which probably demanded a cautious use of the lancet, was subdued, yet the struggle was more dubious than it otherwise would have been. In two instances I had reason to think that full bloodletting was productive of fatal effects. But these were instances of the abuse of bloodletting.

In a patient, in a private practice, to whom I was called on the 10th day of fever, whose face and scalp were injected with dark blood, who lay supine, breathed with stertor, and was insensible, the bowels had resisted the most drastic purgatives, and yet there was no obstruction, no fullness of any part of the abdomen, which on the contrary was remarkably lank. In this case the opening of the temporal artery, from which

the darkest blood flowed, restored the patient for a few hours to the use of his understanding, but next day he died.

Dr. Cheyne.

Report of the Hardwicke Fever Hospital for the year ending on the 31st March, 1818, including a brief account of an Epidemic Fever in Dublin
Dublin Hospital Reports and Communications in Medicine and Surgery
1818

LEECHES AND VENEREAL DISEASE

In the Richmond Surgical Hospital seven small wards are set apart for the reception of male patients labouring under venereal complaints. These wards, which contain beds, are always full, and afford the Surgeons ample opportunities of practice in such cases.

The abstraction of blood from the penis by means of leeches is found extremely useful in many instances, but this should be looked upon purely in the light of an auxiliary remedy and as by no means sufficient to supercede general bloodletting, except in debilitated or unhealthy constitutions. A very general prejudice exists against the application of leeches in these cases, which has originated in an erroneous idea, that the leech-bites are liable to degenerate into venereal ulcers, an occurrence which I have never witnessed; it is true, leech-bites on an inflamed penis do occasionally suppurate, and even ulcerate so as to become very inconvenient to the patient, yet this objection should not deter the practitioner from having recourse to local bloodletting, when severe inflammation, pain and tension of the part indicate its expediency.

Surgical Report; containing an Account of those Affections of the Penis which are generally considered as primary Symptoms of Syphilis, with the Modes of Treatment employed in the Richmond Surgical Hospital
C.H. Todd
1818

VIRILE POWER AND POSTERIOR SCLEROSIS

Another set of reflexes which are often implicated in posterior sclerosis are the vascular reflexes, and chief among these is that concerned in the erection of the penis. The question of virile power in connection with posterior sclerosis was a matter in dispute in the case of Bagot v. Bagot, tried at Dublin in 1878. The testator had by his will denied the legitimacy of his reputed child and the object of the trial was to prove that the will, which partially disinherited the child, was unreasonable. In 1879, Bagot was paraplegic, the result of an injury to the spine. From this he fairly recovered, but, in 1872, he began to manifest symptoms of posterior sclerosis, which were strongly marked a year later and from which he died in 1877, aged 52. In August, 1875, he married a lady who was in the seventh month of pregnancy, and the son and heir was born two months after marriage. At the time when this son was presumably procreated (February, 1875) Bagot was three years advanced in posterior sclerosis and, since he subsequently conceived the idea that the child was not his, it was sought to prove that the posterior sclerosis from which he suffered would, among other things, give support to such a supposition. Only one, among some dozen medical witnesses examined, was of opinion that Bagot's condition was compatible with full virile power, all the others asserted, more or less positively, that impotence was an ordinary concomitant of advanced locomotor ataxy.

Selections from the Clinical Works of Dr. Duchenne De Boulogne
Translated and edited by G.V. Poore
1883

PSYCHIC MESSAGES FROM

OSCAR WILDE

In The Underworld

THE APPEARANCE OF OSCAR WILDE'S GHOST, THROUGH A MEDIUM

"**P**ity, please, lady for poor O.W. in this profundust snobbing I have caught. Nine dirty years mine age, hairs hoar, mummery failend, snowdrift to my ellpow, deff as Adder. I askt you, dear lady, to judge on my tree by our fruits."

Finnegans Wake
James Joyce
1939

COMMUNICATIONS FROM THE OTHER WORLD

Since 1852 there have been literally hundreds of books published which purport to embody communications received from spirits in the other world either through automatic writing, planchette, or the ouija board. Such publications have multiplied enormously, of course, in recent years; but from the very first they have formed a type of literature which is in an extraordinary degree tedious and futile. Between the Scylla of dreary platitude and the Charybdis of flippant puerilities no way seems to have been left open to the unfortunate spirit which desires to communicate from the au-delà*. Some rather striking messages have been received through living-voice mediums, for the most part not long after the death of those who purported to speak; but when great names in the literary world have attempted to rival their earth achievements the results have been deplorable.

And now, after seventy years of frustrated expectation, there comes at last some script which has a distinct literary quality and which appears to be not unworthy of the brilliant writer from whom it purports to emanate.

'The "Oscar Wilde" Script in Its Bearing on Survival'
Herbert Thurston
Studies: An Irish Quarterly Review
March 1924

Hester Travers Smith (1868–1949) was a Dublin-born medium, who spoke to the dead in a professional capacity. She was well known in the literary community, being a close friend of Bram Stoker and W.B. Yeats. She was also friends with the Earl of Oxford, Francis Bacon, and William Shakespeare – all of whom may have been the same person. She is considered to be the inspiration for the medium in Yeats's spiritualist play, *The Words upon the Window Pane*, in which psychic messages are received from the deceased Dean Swift.

AUTOMATIC SCRIPT OBTAINED ON JUNE 8TH, 1923.

SITTERS – MRS. TRAVERS SMITH AND MR. V.

Mrs. T.S Who are you?

Pity Oscar Wilde – one who in the world was a king of life. Bound to Ixion's wheel of thought, I must complete forever the circle of my experience. Long ago, I wrote that there was twilight in my cell and twilight in my heart, but this is the twilight of the soul. In eternal twilight I move, but I know that

---

* The Hereafter

in the world there is day and night, seed time and harvest, and red sunset must follow apple-green dawn. Every year spring throws her green veil over the world and anon the red autumn glory comes to mock the yellow moon. Already the May is creeping like a white mist over lane and hedgerow and year after year the hawthorn bears blood-red fruit after the white death of its May.

– Are you Oscar Wilde?

Yes, Oscar Wilde.

– Tell me the name of the house you lived in in Dublin. Tell me where your father used to practice.

Near Dublin. My father was a surgeon. These names are difficult to recall.

– Not at all difficult if you are really Oscar Wilde.

Oscar Wilde From Purgatory: Psychic Messages
Hester Travers Smith
1923

MR. V, THE AUTOMATIC WRITER

A gentleman, who is still known only as "Mr. V.," had for some time wished to develop the power of automatic writing. He was advised to seek the help of Mrs. Travers Smith, who has had a large experience in this branch of psychic research. She is a daughter of the late Professor Edward Dowden, and was, till recently, well known in Dublin society. At first Mr. V. made little progress, but when Mrs. Travers Smith laid her hand on his while he held the pencil, the pencil began to write intelligent messages.

'The "Oscar Wilde" Script in Its Bearing on Survival'
Herbert Thurston
Studies: An Irish Quarterly Review
March 1924

"MY LITTLE LILY"

At first his pencil tapped repeatedly on the paper, then it began to move more rapidly than at our last meeting. He wrote the name of his deceased friend again; the message concerned his daughter Lily. "I want my daughter Lily, my little Lily," it began. As the word "Lily" was written, I was sensible of an interruption; I felt instinctively that the communicator had changed. I asked who was speaking; immediately "Oscar Wilde" was written and the message continued more and more rapidly. I looked at Mr. V. He seemed only half conscious, his eyes were closed. His pencil was so firmly controlled that I found it very difficult to move it from the end of one line to the beginning of the next. I lifted my hand from his; the pencil stopped instantly; it merely tapped impatiently on the paper.

I was surprised at the clearness and accuracy of the writing. The words were divided, the t's crossed, the i's dotted, even quotation marks were added and punctuation attended to. The signature struck me as unusual and, on reading the script over, I noticed that at times a Greek 'a' was used. Neither Mr. V. nor I had ever seen Wilde's writing so far as we could remember. When he was gone, it struck me that it would be interesting to compare the script with a facsimile, if I could find one. I was singularly fortunate, for, at the Chelsea Book Club, not only did I see a facsimile of Wilde's writing, but an autographed letter of his happened to be there for sale. I was amazed; the handwritings seemed similar.

Oscar Wilde From Purgatory: Psychic Messages
Hester Travers Smith
1923

A COMPARATIVE STUDY OF THE SCRIPT AND WILDE'S ORIGINAL MANUSCRIPTS

I think it will be admitted by those who are familiar with Wilde's descriptive prose, apt at times to be rather flamboyant and over-ornate, that this is, to say the least, a remarkably good parody. Moreover the startling impression thus made was reinforced by another surprising circumstance – the handwriting, though rapid and intense, closely resembled Wilde's. There are several facsimiles of the script given in the articles which have appeared in Psychic Science and, by the kindness of Mrs. Travers Smith, I have also been allowed to inspect at her house several specimens of the script itself. On the other hand, the British Museum possesses the original manuscripts of some of Wilde's plays and poems. I have also consulted these and there can be no possible question as to the close resemblance between the two or, indeed, of the fact that the script aims at reproducing Wilde's handwriting. He had a curious trick of substituting a Greek 'a' for the ordinary small English 'a'.

'The "Oscar Wilde" Script in Its Bearing on Survival'
Herbert Thurston
Studies: An Irish Quarterly Review
March 1924

Sir Arthur Conan Doyle, accompanied

CRITICAL ANALYSIS FROM THE CREATOR OF SHERLOCK HOLMES

Of all forms of mediumship, the highest and most valuable, when it can be relied upon, is that which is called automatic writing, since in this, if the form be pure, we seem to have found a direct method of obtaining teaching from the Beyond. Unhappily, it is a method which lends itself very readily to self-deception, since it is certain that the subconscious mind of man has many powers with which we are as yet imperfectly acquainted. It is impossible ever to accept any automatic script whole-heartedly as a hundred per cent statement of truth from the Beyond. The stained glass will still tint the light which passes through it and our human organism will never be crystal clear. The verity of any particular specimen of such writing must depend not upon mere assertion, but upon corroborative details and the general dissimilarity from the mind of the writer and similarity to that of the alleged inspirer. When, for example, in the case of the late Oscar Wilde, you get long communications which are not only characteristic of his style, but which contain constant allusions to obscure episodes in his own life and which finally are written in his own handwriting, it must be admitted that the evidence is overpoweringly strong.

The History of Spiritualism
Sir Arthur Conan Doyle
1926

COPY OF COMMUNICATION RECEIVED AT THE OUIJA BOARD BY MRS. TRAVERS SMITH, JULY 12TH, 1923.

RECORDED BY MISS CUMMINS.

Oscar at your bidding, dear lady.

– Do you object to speaking of your prison life?

I do not at all object to speaking to you about what was to me a most enthralling experience. When I say enthralling I mean that my circuit of the world's pain would not have been adequate without that supreme misery, for to me it was supreme. I, who worshipped beauty, was robbed not only of the chance of beholding her face, but I was cast in on myself; and there, in that barrenness of soul, I languished until my spirit rose once more and cried aloud that this was its great opportunity.

    Oscar, dear lady, waits for you. My soul was healing, but my vision of things seen was blind. What service are the eyes if they behold nothing but bare and ugly walls and barer, uglier humanity?

Oscar Wilde From Purgatory: Psychic Messages
Hester Travers Smith
1923

8. Mount Street
Grosvenor Square.

Dear Mr. Young,

I have only just returned from Paris, or would have done myself the pleasure of communicating sooner with you. I will be very glad if I can be of any service to the author of Pendragon, and if you have no better engagement perhaps you will breakfast with me, sans façon, tomorrow (Friday) at 11 o'c.

most truly yours
Oscar Wilde.

LETTER TO THE EDITOR

When I consider the various corroborations in this case of Oscar Wilde:

1) The reproduction of his heavy style;
2) The reproduction of his light style;
3) The reproduction of character;
4) The recollection of incidents, some of them quite obscure, in his own life;
5) The reproduction of his handwriting;
6) And (at least in my eyes) the similarity of the conditions

which he describes upon the other side with those which our psychic knowledge would assign to such a man, I consider that the case is a very powerful one indeed.

It is difficult to note these close analogies of style and to doubt that an Oscar Wilde brain is at the back of it.

Sir Arthur Conan Doyle

Occult Review
Volume 39, April 1924

COPY OF AUTOMATIC SCRIPT OBTAINED MONDAY, JUNE 18TH, 1923.

Present.-Mr. V., Mrs. Travers Smith, Mr. B., Mr. Dingwall (Research Officer of the Society for Psychical Research), Miss Cummins.

MR. V. WAS THE AUTOMATIST, MRS. T.S. TOUCHING HIS HAND.

Being dead is the most boring experience in life. That is, if one excepts being married or dining with a schoolmaster. Do you doubt my identity? I am not surprised, since sometimes I doubt it myself. I might retaliate by doubting yours.

Fortunately, there are no facts over here. On earth we could scarcely escape them. Their dead carcasses were strewn everywhere on the rose path of life. One could not pick up a newspaper without learning something useful. In it were some sordid statistics of crime or disgusting detail relating to the consumption of pork that met the eyes or we were told with a precision that was perfectly appalling and totally unnecessary – What time the moon had decided to be jealous and eclipse the sun.

Shall we ask him some questions?

Don't degrade me into giving you facts.

Oscar Wilde From Purgatory: Psychic Messages
Hester Travers Smith
1923

LETTER TO THE EDITOR
THE STRANGE CASE OF OSCAR WILDE

I maintain that a person might possess the power to imitate Wilde in his capacity of essayist and wit and yet be entirely destitute of his power of inventing a plot or a faculty for telling a story. The mere production of epigram and decorative prose by no means exhausts the literary versatility of the real Wilde, who, besides being a clever playwright and excellent classical scholar, was in addition a born story-teller.

C.W. Soal

Occult Review
Volume 39, March 1924

THE LITERARY OPINIONS OF OSCAR WILDE'S GHOST

It may surprise you to learn that in this way I have dipped into the works of some of your modern novelists. That is, I have not drawn the whole brew, but tasted the vintage. You have much to learn.

On Arnold Bennett: The assiduous apprentice to literature, who has conjured so long with the wand of his master Flaubert that he has really succeeded in persuading himself and others that he has learnt the trick. But Flaubert's secret is far from him.

On John Galsworthy: The only mind I have entered into which appeals to my literary sense is John Galsworthy. He is my successor.

On Thomas Hardy: A very harmless writer, Hardy. I well remember how his Tess set maiden hearts a-throbbing. It was a tale which might attract the schoolgirl who imagined she had just arrived at puberty.

On George Meredith: He had a most ingenious way of plaiting words, so that his most ardent admirers could never extricate his thoughts from them. They clung about his ideas as barnacles on an old ship. And he was so completely clogged that his ideas escaped and only words were left.

On George Moore: One difficulty, in reading him, is to differentiate between the sexes. I am ever intrigued as to whether his men are women or his women men. Thus Moore murmurs on; never a clear or masculine idea, but the half-tone, delicately sexless, sustained throughout.

On H.G. Wells: Time will ruthlessly prune Mr. Wells' fig trees.

– What is your opinion of Bernard Shaw?

Shaw, after all, might be called a contemporary of mine. We had almost reached the point of rivalry, in a sense, when I was taken from the scene of action. I had a kindly feeling towards poor Shaw. He had such a keen desire to be original that it moved my pity. He is so anxious to prove himself honest and outspoken that he utters a great deal more than he is able to think. He cannot analyse, he is merely trying to overturn the furniture and laughs with delight when he sees the canvas bottoms of the chairs he has flung over.

– What is your opinion of "Ulysses"* by James Joyce?

Yes, I have smeared my fingers with that vast work. It has given me one exquisite moment of amusement. I gathered that if I hoped to retain my reputation as an intelligent shade, open to new ideas, I must peruse this volume. It is a singular matter that a countryman of mine should have produced this great bulk of filth. You may smile at me for uttering thus when you reflect that, in the eyes of the world, I am a tainted creature. But, at least, I had a sense of the values of things on the terrestrial globe. Here in "Ulysses," I find a monster who cannot contain the monstrosities of his own brain. The creatures he gives birth to leap from him in shapeless masses of hideousness, as dragons might, which in their foulsome birth contaminate their parent ... This book appeals to all my senses. It gratifies the soil which is in every one of us. It gives me the impression of having been written in a severe fit of

nausea. Surely there is a nausea fever. The physicians may not have diagnosed it. But here, we have the heated vomit continued through the countless pages of this work. The author thought, no doubt, that he had given the world a series of ideas. Ideas which had sprung from out his body, not his mind!

I feel that if this work has caught a portion of the public, who may take it for the truth, that I, even I, who am a shade, and I who have tasted the fullness of life and its mead of bitterness, should cry aloud:

---

* "Note. About a year previous to this sitting Mrs. Travers Smith had glanced at a copy of "Ulysses" for a few minutes in Ireland. Out of seven hundred pages she could not have read more than half a dozen, nor had she read reviews of this work. So she was not in a position to criticize it."

"Shame upon Joyce, shame on his work, shame on his lying soul."

-You are most amusing.

I am glad that a poor ghost can bring laughter to your eyes.

Oscar Wilde From Purgatory: Psychic Messages
Hester Travers Smith
1923

Geraldine Cummins (1890–1969) was Travers Smith's frequent assistant during the Wilde sittings. Born in Cork, she made a life for herself among the literary circles of Dublin. Although she was herself a spirit medium, she was better known as a novelist and playwright, finding some success in the Abbey Theatre. In both facets of her professional life, she employed automatic writing.

MY PERSONAL BACKGROUND

The technique of composition has always been of deep interest to me, and when I was a young Irishwoman it developed on two lines. (1) The composition was the creation of my conscious mind. (2) It was derived from the unconscious. In the former case, I write very slowly and laboriously and have to revise the MS again and again. A short story has taken my conscious mind a month to compose. To be of any literary value, my published stories and novels and one biography have had to be about Irish characters and my native country Ireland. On the conscious mind level, I have tried and failed to write about English people. I did not know them sufficiently well to make their characters come alive in fiction. They remained foreigners to me.

But when my writing was derived from the unconscious, it has been a very different affair. The theme was never Ireland or the Irish people. For instance, certain English and American persons' characters and personalities, unknown to me, were reported by their relatives or friends to have been successfully delineated in such writing. Its composition emerged from the deeper levels of mind, so much so it seemed as if I were merely a secretary taking down an already fully composed narrative by another author and my pen travelled over page after page with abnormal rapidity. Various authors, notably William Blake the poet, have had that strange experience of dictated writing. We cannot explain it. But in my case such transmitted writing (a more correct term than 'automatic writing') led me into psychical research.

I use the adjective transmitted to define it because my conscious mind is suspended, plays no part in the communication. Whatever the source of such writings, i.e. a subconscious or a common unconscious mind or a discarnate individual's mind I have not composed a single sentence of those rapidly written scripts when provided.

Swan on a Black Sea
Geraldine Cummins
1965

"BRILLIANT FLASHES"

There are many brilliant flashes in the Wilde script which are quite in the tone of cynical paradox which runs through such an essay as "The Decay of Lying." Take, for instance, the following, which was obtained by Mr. V., when working with another medium, a Mrs. L., who, I understand, is not identical with the famous Mrs. Osborne Leonard.

Mrs. L., much excited, remarks to Mr. V. : "You know I am not guiding your hand. I am perfectly honest."

The hand writes immediately: "Honesty, madam, may be the best policy for the grocer, but it is the very worst for a woman with a past."

Mrs. L.: "Oscar Wilde! How dare you! What can you know of my life?"

"Pray don't be angry... Charming women always have a past, and plain women never have a future."

Mrs. L.: "Thanks for the compliment, but I assure you I have been very moderate in my follies, very moderate indeed."

"... Ah, moderation! We do in moderation the things we don't like and, in excess, the things other people don't like us to do. That is all."

'The "Oscar Wilde" Script in Its Bearing on Survival'
Herbert Thurston
Studies: An Irish Quarterly Review
March 1924

In a special sitting for the *Sunday Express*, Mrs. Travers-Smith asked Wilde about a recent busman's holiday they took with her spirit-guide, Johannes.

– Did you come with me to the Haymarket Theatre to see *"The Importance of Being Earnest"* last Thursday?

It was a most amusing experience. I looked through your eyes and saw my children again and realised for the first time that they were merely marionettes, not human beings. You, who have an idea of what the value of humour is, could hardly grasp, as I could, the attitude of the audience that night. I was pleased to note in their laughter a feeling that, after all, although he had made mistakes in his life, he could still entertain. I could see a slightly contemptuous colour in these minds. They felt that he was a shade démodé, but they looked on him as a curio worthy of a dark corner in the drawing-room.

The author is very grateful to the management and cast for putting his poor ideas again before the public. He finds it difficult to enter into the present time. But so far as he is permitted to see the Haymarket production, it is smartened beyond his powers and given to the present day with a sauce which should make it palatable to all.

I feel now that it would be futile to write a comedy. My own little play is so totally away from its own element that I should like to cover up the poor little nursling and lead it away from the footlights. They make its colours pale and dim. A sad little effort this, to revive the feelings of a different age.

– Will you go on with the new play?

I have been considering it, and it is certain it will be written, and in a manner different from my poor little "Earnest."

In 1928, Travers Smith announced that Wilde had dictated a play to her, the unproduced *Is it a Forgery?*

The "Oscar Wilde" script which I offer to the public, both because of its literary and psychic interest, seems to me to suggest definitely the possibility that we may be in touch with an external influence. If I were fully convinced of that fact, I should certainly be as fully convinced that Oscar Wilde had spoken to the world again. I should not attribute any messages so characteristic of the whole man to an impersonation on the other side. I think, in this case, it is a choice of two hypotheses; either Oscar Wilde is speaking or the whole script, ouija board, and automatic writing must be derived from the subconsciousness or clairvoyance of two mediums. In either case, the matter of the messages and the manner in which they came are of such unusual interest that I feel the entire case should he stated as fully as possible. I believe it to be quite outside those which can be accused of being trivial or dull.

Oscar Wilde From Purgatory: Psychic Messages
Hester Travers Smith
1923

ON FABRICATION

But the reader will probably ask: may not the whole thing be a fake, a practical joke? Would it not have been easy for Mr. V. to write or to procure some clever parodies of Oscar Wilde's dithyrambs and inverted aphorisms, to learn them by heart, to study and carefully practise his handwriting and then, after a pretence of unsuccessful experiments in automatism, to invoke the assistance of Mrs. Travers Smith and at the psychological moment to pour them out at lightning speed for the mystification of the credulous?

'The "Oscar Wilde" Script in Its Bearing on Survival'
Herbert Thurston
Studies: An Irish Quarterly Review
March 1924

It demands a very wide stretch of imagination to believe that sub-conscious memory from a possible glance at Wilde's writing could produce hundreds of pages of script which never varies in its imitation and is written in a handwriting which is totally unlike Mr. V.'s or mine. Most of those facts, which were unknown to the mediums, but which I have verified as being correct, came in automatic writing.

Oscar Wilde From Purgatory: Psychic Messages
Hester Travers Smith
1923

However, I must confess that such an elaborate mystification seems to me, on the whole, improbable; first, because, in view of the amount of script obtained through Mr. V. and the rapidity with which it comes, the effort of memory would be a very astounding feat; secondly, because where questions are asked it would be difficult to foresee them and provide

Wildean answers beforehand; but thirdly, and more particularly, because Mrs. Travers Smith, unassisted, obtains script through the ouija board which equally purports to come from Oscar Wilde and which is said to be not inferior in quality. Of Mrs. Travers Smith's honesty I can entertain no doubt.

'The "Oscar Wilde" Script in Its Bearing on Survival'
Herbert Thurston
Studies: An Irish Quarterly Review
March 1924

THE FOLLOWING COMMUNICATION CAME THROUGH MRS. TRAVERS SMITH'S HAND AT THE OUIJA BOARD, JULY 5TH, 1923.

Recorded by Miss Cummins. It was with difficulty the recorder kept pace with the message.

– I have a question to ask.

Your question shall have my best attention, if it savours of what concerns yourself; if it concerns me, I reserve the right to be silent if necessary.

– Why did you select me as your medium?

That, my dear lady, is not easy to explain. I have told you how I gazed through the eyes of many nations, that I might gain once more a look into the glory of the world. I had often fancied conveying my thoughts from this place of darkness to someone who had a fitting understanding of a mind such as mine is – fantastical and pained by a desire to express beauty in words. I tried many times to secure a vial for my ideas, which could contain them in an essence as it were. But until the day when I seized the pencil from some unnoticeable being, who seemed to make an effort to press through the brain of "the tool," never before had I found the exact quality I needed. If I am to speak again as I used, or to use the pen, I must have a clear brain to work with. It must let my thoughts flow through as fine sand might, if filtered through a glass cylinder. It must be clear and there must be material which I can make use of. I can use the hand of the tool and leave an impress of my writing as I used.

Oscar Wilde From Purgatory: Psychic Messages
Hester Travers Smith
1923

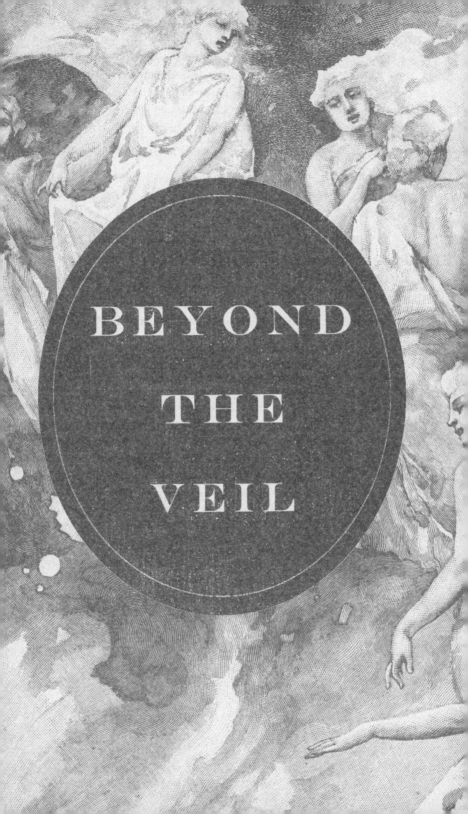

BEYOND

THE

VEIL

Mrs. Travers Smith was not alone in her creative pursuits. She moved through turn-of-the-century Dublin literary circles and, as is usual after joining a circle, all its members clasped hands and held a séance. Books were dictated through automatic writing; poems were dredged up from visionistic trance-states; even Somerville & Ross, authors of *The Irish R.M.*, claimed to continue their collaboration from beyond one contributor's grave.

While science and art seem so often at angles to each other, on this occasion they formed another circle: artists took part in psychical experiments and physicists had visions. There were mystic societies and scientific groups and their memberships overlapped. Art and science joined hands and asked a question of the dark: what will death be like?

THE MODERN MINDSET

What a change in the last twenty years! The weird legends of our childhood are vanishing; their superstitious glamour, which we are both glad and sorry to lose, is being replaced by the conscientiously gathered minutiae of the scientific investigators ... This scientific age is realistic in its ghost stories. Mr. Wallace catches a small sprite at work in a hinged slate; Mr. Crookes photographs one by the electric light ... When the haunts of the "Krakens" of the supernatural are found, science will have some fun and we may expect some good stories.

On W.F. Barrett's 'The Demons of Derrygonnelly'
Dublin University Magazine
1879

SPIRITUALISM IN DUBLIN, IRELAND.

BY IVER MacDONNELL.

Spiritualism, so far as I am aware, was first introduced into Dublin about fourteen years ago, by Capt. Casement — a gentleman who took much interest in the subject and brought an uneducated medium from Lancashire, named Alexander. Neither the table-moving manifestations of this medium nor the persuasion of the captain had any influence beyond exciting a temporary interest with a few and producing contempt and ridicule with most who witnessed his experiments.

I obtained a private sitting with him; when it was intimated by a female spirit, in reply to my question as to her reason of coming to me, "You will yet be the means of forwarding this truth in Ireland."

A course of study and practice of mesmerism prepared me for receiving the experiments of the Davenport Brothers as genuine some time after, in the early part of 1866. Struck by their phenomena, I formed a circle of the members of my family and a few friends and succeeded in developing three writing-mediums:— one a gentleman, through whom the spirits of Charlotte Brontë and of the poet Shelley purported to communicate.

On all occasions, I invited inquirers of all sorts to be present, several of whom formed circles of their own afterwards. And so, the subject is fairly started in Dublin, but, as yet, utterly disbelieved by the public; while the adherents may be included in a couple of dozen.

Ireland will yet be, I believe, a grand field for Spiritualism, as its people have ever been truly religious. The very superstitions so abundant in its history, the fairy-lore, the charms, the miraculous power of relics, &c, prove the existence of the mind susceptible to this science, as contrasted with the metaphysical, reasoning head of the Scotchman, and the materialistic, matter-of-fact, sensuous character of the Englishman.

Dublin Review
October 1867

THE BROTHERS DAVENPORT IN DUBLIN

O n the first day of the New Year, 1866, early in the morning, I, in company with the Davenports and Mr. Fay, arrived in Dublin.

We established ourselves at the Queen's Arms Hotel, Sackville Street, and made arrangements for giving a séance there. For this purpose, invitations were sent to the Press and several influential gentlemen, some of whom were connected with Trinity College. About forty attended. I said we came before them to submit facts on which everyone was capable of exercising his faculties and forming his own judgement — that we offered no theories and called upon them to indulge in or accept no fancies, but simply to witness a number of facts which would be put before them without mystery or disguise.

The usual manifestations took place and were witnessed with astonishment and caused much speculation.

Mr. Trail, a man of note at Trinity College, entered the cabinet with the Brothers and, on emerging from it, exclaimed "That's grand by Jove." One of the Editors of the *Irish Times* also entered the cabinet and reported favourably

The Brothers Davenport in performance

NOTICE!

At the conclusion of the

CABINET SEANCE

OF THE

DAVENPORT BROTHERS

MR. WILLIAM M. FAY

Who has travelled with the Davenport Brothers for the past nine years, will give what is termed a special

"DARK SEANCE"

To a limited number of Ladies and Gentlemen. The extraordinary wonders that occur in the Dark Seance are universally considered to far transcend anything witnessed in the Public Cabinet Seance of the Brothers. The peculiar nature of the experiments, the bewildering, mysterious and astonishing results produced, have been pronounced by those who have witnessed them to be unrivalled. The eccentric movements of the various instruments, the marvellous rapidity with which they are seen flying through space, the astounding experiment with Mr. Fay's Coat, as it is seen leaving his back and flying through the air, and other curious experiences, all of which must be seen to be realized.

Cards of Admission to this Special Seance by Mr. Fay can be procured at the conclusion of the Davenport Seance,

PRICE, - - - $1.00

F. A. Searle, Printer Joannes Building (up one flight), 110 Washington Street.

of his experience. The Dark Séance followed and went off equally satisfactory.

A profound impression was obviously made on the company which included two Rev. D.D.s., one of whom, Rev. Dr. Tisdal, offered his coat to be put on Mr. Fay. This gentleman, considering his position, which was that of the most popular and fashionable clergyman in Dublin, acted a bold and manly part. He not only stood up for the facts, but proclaimed them far and wide and wrote in the public papers in defence of the Davenports when their integrity was assailed. The next morning, long and favourable notices appeared in all the papers and an excitement was created that, for the time, threw Fenianism into the shade.

To convey an idea of the favourable impression produced by the first séance, I give some extracts from the articles that appeared. The *Freeman's Journal*, after describing the phenomena witnessed, sums up thus:–

"Suffice it to say that we witnessed the strangest and most unaccountable performance that could be thought of next to the sacred miracles. They certainly succeeded in astonishing all who had the pleasure of attending their soiree yesterday evening."

The *Irish Times* has the following sensible remarks to begin with:–

"The Davenports, respecting whom so much has been written, have visited Dublin and, last evening, held a séance in the Queen's Arms Hotel, Upper Sackville Street. That they are possessed with mysterious power, bordering almost on the supernatural, would appear to be undoubted. The phenomena which they present astound the audience and defy all efforts at discovery. Mystery of the darkest description pervades the entire performance to such an extent that the sceptical were almost induced to abandon scepticism and join in the very extravagant and absurd opinion that the phenomena presented were the result of a supernatural agency."

Saunder's *Newsletter and Daily Advertiser* says of the first Séance:–
"For three hours, we were in an atmosphere pervaded with mystery and wonder that, long 'ere the performance was over, we had given up all hope of finding the key to anything we saw."

Spiritual Experiences: including Seven Months with the Brothers Davenport
Robert Cooper
1867

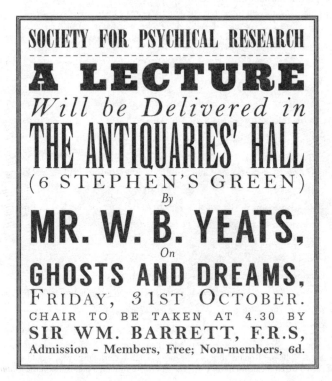

Iver MacDonnell was correct that Ireland – and Dublin especially – would prove a grand field for Spiritualism, and it soon housed many interested scientists and mystics.

Best known among the latter was **W.B. Yeats** (1865–1839), the Nobel Laureate, whose prose, plays, and poems make frequent use of spiritist and mystic themes and techniques. Yeats freely joined the many magick orders and lodges of Ireland and Britain and he welcomed into his home the most interesting of the internationally renowned mediums.

AN EARL PASSES

Brailey* sat quietly in a chair looking over Dublin Bay from the windows of our drawing room. When the writing ceased, the clairvoyant said he had not the slightest impression of what was behind it, probably because his attention had been caught by what appeared to be a special event taking place over the hill (Howth) across the water. A procession in archaic costumes circled in the air just above the hill. It was not a joyous procession, but sorrowful. We could throw no light on the phenomenon. Next day's newspaper announced the death of the Earl of Howth, the last of an ancient line of Irish nobility.

We Two Together
J.H. & M.E. Cousins
1950

---

* This was William "Ronald" Brailey, the famed English spiritualist, who would subsequently foretell the death of his own son, Theodore Brailey, a pianist upon the *Titanic*

THE PIG

The medium squatted on the carpet, appeared to go into a trance, and addressed himself in the broken English of an alleged Red Indian "control" to Yeats and Miss Gonne. They were accompanied, the control said, by a tall, bearded man, over whom a flag connected with Ireland flew. Further than the description of the form the control could not go. Name and identity were beyond his knowledge. Then he saw a picture, a pig. But he exclaimed, this was no ordinary pig. "This pig had shot himself!"*

We Two Together
J.H. & M.E. Cousins
1950

AN EXPLANATION OF LIFE

Like every other student of the subject, I have been bewildered by the continual deceits, by the strange dream-like manifestations, by the continual fraud. Why, e.g., does Miss "Burton" when she is entranced commit ingenious frauds which deceive not only the sitters, but Miss Burton when she is awake? Why is that when Albert de Rochas asks his sensitives to go back into past lives & tell him who they were they can sometimes describe scenery, names, families even, that they have never heard of in their waking state, & yet claim to be people whose existence can be disproved? Why this mixture of reality, of messages that seem to come precisely as they say they do from the dead, with messages that but express the thoughts of the living?

A Vision: An Explanation of Life Founded upon the Writings of Giraldus and upon Certain Doctrines Attributed to Kusta Ben Luka
W.B. Yeats
1925

---

* It was understood, by all in attendance, that this was a reference to Richard Piggott, an anti-Parnellite, who forged letters implying Parnell's involvement in the Phoenix Park murders, before taking his own life in a hotel room in Madrid.

Hester Travers Smith and George William Russell (Æ), 1934

  IMMORTALITY

We must pass like smoke, or live within the spirits' fire;
  For we can no more than smoke unto the flame return.
If our thought has changed to dream, or will into desire,
  As smoke we vanish o'er the fires that burn.

Lights of infinite pity star the grey dusk of our days;
  Surely here is soul; with it we have eternal breath;
In the fire of love we live or pass by many ways,
  By unnumbered ways of dream to death.

Æ
The *Irish Theosophist*
July 15th, 1894

THE SPECTRUM OF IRISH THEOSOPHISTS

Annie Besant, second International President of the Theosophical
Society (1907–1933); James Cousins, playwright; Margaret Cousins,

Charles Johnston (middle back) with the Blavatsky family

suffragette; Charles Johnston, founder of the Dublin lodge in 1886*;
W.B. Yeats; William Quan Judge, founding member of the Theosophical
Society and headed the first Society in America; Maud MacCarthy, violinist
and authority on Indian music; Æ (George William Russell), poet and
artist; Ella Young, poet and mythologist.

A Word Upon the Objects of the Theosophical Society – by Æ

1st:—To form the nucleus of a Universal Brotherhood of Humanity, without
distinction of race, creed, sex, caste or colour.

2nd:—To promote the study of Aryan and other Eastern literatures, religions,
philosophies and sciences, and demonstrate the importance of that study.

3rd:—To investigate unexplained laws of nature and the psychic powers
latent in man.

The *Irish Theosophist*
November 15th, 1892

---

*   Johnston and Yeats formed the Dublin Hermetic Society in June 1885, of which Yeats
was president. A fortnight later, Johnston travelled to London, where he met Madame
Blavatsky, the founder of the Theosophy movement and, in time, his aunt-in-law. On
his return to Dublin, he suggested that the Hermetic Society become the Dublin Lodge
of Theosophy, which Yeats resisted. The transition took place in April 1886, when the
Hermetic Society was dissolved. Yeats refused to join the new organisation until much later
that year, when his resolve to join no other orders weakened.

THEOSOPHY AND THEOSOPHIST

Mr. W.T. Brown, B.A., Professor of Constitutional History, Jusiprudence, and Political Economy in University College, Dublin.

The "Society for Psychical Research," is an association of well-meaning ladies and gentlemen, some of them having a reputation for learning. It owes its existence to the curiosity excited by Theosophy and other cults of the kind. Professor Sidgwick of Cambridge, Professor Barrett of Dublin, and other Psychical Researchers, were puzzled by the marvels of Thibetan magic and they resolved to test, to the best of their ability, the pretentions of the magicians. To a great many persons their conscientious inquiries may have seemed superfluous – a waste of useful energy upon a transparently worthless subject. But they deserve whatever praise is due to the exposure of a delusion, which deluded no one except the utterly fatuous.

The *Lyceum*
November 1889

DEBATE AT THE ABBEY THEATRE

Mr. W.B. Yeats said that he did not care whether the audience believed in good or bad spirits. His object was to impress upon them that there was very strong reason for believing that living persons were in constant communication with the other world. The position of those who did not believe in these phenomena was shaken from the point of view of science and they were heretics from the point of view of the Church to which they belonged. He thought that this country should make up its mind for itself and have an Irish point of view. He did not think that Ireland should take a casual international attitude about anything. There were people in this country who were constantly seeing various forms of supernatural existence — something that had to be accounted for. He was not urging any person to go and see a séance. It needed a very well-balanced mind and a great deal of knowledge for people to test the phenomena. It was far better to leave psychical research to people who had made it the business of their lives, there were so many chances of being deceived. (Hear! hear!) They were trying to convince the ordinary man who was, unfortunately, not susceptible of philosophical or theological arguments that a man does not go out like a candle when he dies. The scepticism of the modern world came from the fact that man is blinded by physical science. The man who believes in nothing (said Mr. Yeats) has made the world poisonous to live in and he objected to living in that world, if he could do anything to change it.

Irish Times
February 3rd, 1919

THE SPECTRUM OF MEMBERSHIP OF THE SOCIETY FOR PSYCHICAL RESEARCH, DUBLIN SECTION, CIRCA. 1908.

Vice Provost Barlow, Chairman of the Section; Professor Barrett, F.R.S., Vice-Chairman of the Section; Lady Lyttleton; Lady Gregory; Sir Archibald Gelkie; Dean Bernard, the Bishop of Meath; Miss Whita, LL.D; Mrs. T.W. Russell; Mr. E.E. Fournier d'Albe, Hon Secretary of the Section; Sir Lambert Ormsby; Miss Barrett; Mrs. Fournier d'Albe; Dr. Bruce; Commissioner Bailey; Mr. Wellington Darley and Mrs. Darley; Lady Dockrell; Mr. J.E. Gore; Miss M. Guinness; Mrs. Jonathan Hogg; Mrs. Deemster Gill; Mrs. J.H. Cousins; Mr. and Mrs. T.W. Rolleston; Mrs. Vanston; Mrs. Trouton; Mrs. Wilkins; Mr. C.H. Oldham; Mrs. S. O'Grady; Mrs. G. Coffet; Miss Gleeson; Mr. C.J. Wilson; the Rev. C.W. O'Hara Mease; Mr. A.C. MacGregor.

THIS AFTERNOON, at 4 p.m., PROFESSOR BARRETT, F.R.S., will lecture in St. Peter's Schoolhouse, Camden Row. The Dean of St. Patrick's will preside.

The lecture will deal specially with apparitions after death and automatic writing. The interest of this second lecture will be enhanced by a few experiments with which Professor Barrett will illustrate some scientific principles bearing on the subject.

Irish Times
March 25th, 1909

The Dublin Section of the Society for Psychical Research was founded by **Sir William Fletcher Barrett** (1844–1925), Professor of Experimental Physics at the Royal College of Science for Ireland, who first became interested in the paranormal upon meeting a Meath man, John Wilson, at the Royal Institution.

The Society was started with a view to examining allegedly paranormal phenomena in a scientific and unbiased way. As a result, it counted among its members as many scientists and sceptics as believers.

SOME EXPERIMENTS CONDUCTED AT BARRETT'S KINGSTOWN HOME, WITH A CIRCLE OF HIS CLOSE FRIENDS

TELEPATHY

In 1882, some careful experiments were made by me in my own house at Kingstown, Co. Dublin. Here the subject was a lad named Fearnley and the hypnotizer, a complete stranger to him, was a friend, Mr. G. A. Smith.

On one of two precisely similar cards I wrote the word "Yes" and on the other "No." Placing the hypnotized subject or percipient so that he could not see the cards I held, a request was made that he would open his hand if the card "Yes" was shown to the agent, Mr. Smith, or not open it if "No." was pointed to. In this way Mr. Smith, who was not in contact with the percipient, silently willed in accordance with the card shown to him.

The percipient remained throughout motionless, with eyes closed and apparently asleep in an arm-chair in one corner of my study; it is needless to repeat that, even had he been wide awake, he had no means whatever of seeing which card was selected by me. Here are the results, with varying distances between the agent, Mr. Smith, and the percipient, Fearnley.

Distance	Successes	Failures
3ft	25	0
6ft	6	0
12ft	6	0
17ft	6	0

A final experiment was made when Mr. Smith was taken across the hall and placed in the dining-room, at a distance of about 30 feet from the subject, two doors, both quite closed, intervening. Under these conditions three trials were made with success, the "Yes" response being, however, very faint and hardly audible to me when I returned to the study to ask the usual question after handing the card to the distant operator. At this point, the subject fell into a deep sleep and made no further replies to the questions addressed to him.

OUIJA BOARD

A small private circle of friends of mine in Dublin have devoted themselves for a few years past to experiments with the Ouija board and have obtained some remarkable results. A joint paper by myself and one of the sitters — the

Rev. Savill Hicks, M.A. — was read by the latter before the S.P.R. wherein some of the communications were given.

The sitters found, when they were carefully blindfolded, that the indicator moved with as great ease and precision as when they could see the letters of the alphabet. Questions were promptly answered and the indicator often moved so rapidly that their hands had some difficulty in keeping pace with it: in fact the recorder who took down the communications had frequently to resort to shorthand.

I asked could any friend of mine communicate; a message was spelt out from a deceased friend, whom I will call Sir John Hartley, giving his full Christian and surname correctly, and he sent a message to the Dublin "Grand Lodge of Freemasons." Sir John when on earth had held a very high rank in the Masonic order, though this fact was quite unknown to the sitters.

I then asked one of the sitters to allow me to take his place and this I did after being securely blindfolded. On putting my fingers on the indicator, along with the two other sitters, the extraordinary vigour, decision, and swiftness with which the indicator moved startled me and it seemed incredible that any coherent message could be in process of delivery. But the recorder had taken down the message which came as follows:

"The same combination must always work together in order to obtain the important messages, as it is very tiring unless the same three are present; there is one present who is unsuited for the receiving."

The recorder asked who this was and was told that it referred to myself! It was not until we removed the bandages from our eyes that any of the sitters knew the purport of the messages given.

PROPHETIC MESSAGES

I have given these details to establish the fact that, whatever may have been the source of the intelligence displayed, it was absolutely beyond the range of any normal human faculty. As for the numerous messages that came through the blindfolded sitters, one from the control, Isaac David Solomon, on October 19th, 1912, — just after the first Balkan war had broken out — was as follows:

"Blood, blood everywhere in the near East. A great nation will fall and a small nation will rise. A great religion will stand in danger. Blood everywhere. News that will astonish the civilised world will come to hand within the next week."

Now, whatever the source of this message, it was perfectly true, for within a week afterwards the first victory of the Bulgarians at Kirk Kilisse was announced and later on, as we know, a great nation (Turkey) fell and a small nation (Bulgaria) rose; whilst more recently Europe has been drenched in blood.

THE MYSTERY OF PETER ROONEY

This control passed and the American-Irishman, Peter Rooney, persistently intruded himself and told us the story of his life and recent death. The purport of it was that he had lived a wretched and bad life, mostly in gaol, and, he added, life at last became so unendurable that ten days previously he threw himself under a tramcar in Boston and so committed suicide. It was only afterwards that the blindfolded sitters knew the purport of the message, they were laughing and chatting together during its delivery.

To us lookers-on, it seemed very incongruous, for the message was delivered in the most life-like manner, with evident pain and reluctance leading up to the tragic conclusion.

The next day I wrote to the Governor of the State Prison at Boston, Mass., to the Chief of Police in that city, to the Chief of Police at Boston, Lincolnshire, to the distinguished corresponding member of the S.P.R., Dr. Morton Prince, of Boston, U.S.A., and to Dr. Hyslop, Hon. Sec. of the American S.P.R., asking if any information could be given to me concerning this Peter Rooney and requesting a reply as soon as possible.

In the course of a few weeks, I obtained answers to my enquiries. No man of this name was known at Boston in England; no Peter Rooney had been in confinement at Boston Prison, Mass.; and no former inmate of that prison had recently committed suicide. The chief Inspector of Police at Boston, Mass., made a thorough investigation and found that no Peter Rooney had been sent to prison from Boston or had been committed to the Reformatory or had committed suicide.

Dr. Morton Prince, of Boston, however, obtained from the Police Records of Boston that a Peter Rooney had fallen from the elevated railway in Boston in August 1910, had received a scalp wound, was attended by a

Sir William Barrett

doctor, laid up for a month, and was still living in his home, York Street, Boston. It was probably only a chance coincidence that a man of the same name had met with an accident in Boston.

Psychical Research
Sir William F. Barrett
1911

ANNOUNCEMENT OF DEATH

The late Sir William Barrett had planned a book on Deathbed Visions, which his sudden death prevented him from finishing. Messrs. Methuen now publish it at 3s. 6d., edited so well that no gaps are apparent. The subject is an important and interesting one. At the opening of the drains of the afterlife, it is interesting to read of what men and women see and hear before the curtains are drawn apart.

The *Spectator*
June 11th, 1926

SPIRITUALISM CRITICISED
DANGER TO THE NERVOUS SYSTEM

To a large audience yesterday evening, Rev. Professor A.H. McNeile, D.D., Regius Professor of Divinity in the University of Dublin continued his series of lectures on the Problem of the Future Life.

One fact which had proved up to the hilt was that spiritualism was attended with great danger. Many brain and nerve experts had vied with each other in this conviction. Scientific investigators were immune from the danger exactly in proportion as their attitude was scientific and impartial, but people who were not scientific and who desired to get into touch with loved ones or to enjoy bizarre and uncanny sensations were drawn into it without knowledge enough to guard them from illusion and deception. They were liable to various forms of neurosis not infrequently leading in the direction of insanity and sometimes, with this deterioration and moral depravity, the greatest peril of all was that of the medium, as Sir William Barrett stated, owing to the weakening of the self control and personal responsibility.

The *Age*
May 13th, 1925

GONE TO ANOTHER WORLD
PETER GANNON'S DELIBERATE PREPARATIONS FOR DEATH.

One of the most remarkable letters ever left by a person having committed suicide for perusal by the Coroners of this City was submitted in evidence yesterday at an inquest held by Coroner Brady.

Subjoined are extracts from it:

"New-York, Aug. 27, 1881.

To Whom it may Concern:

My name is Peter Gannon. I was born in the City of Dublin, in 1851, and am now a citizen of the United States. This is a second time within a month that I have attempted to end my earthly life. The other attempt was made on the evening of Thursday Aug. 15. and was, accountably to me, unsuccessful. I procured a hypodermic syringe and, after considerable trouble, five grains of morphine. I dissolved three grains, but in getting it in the syringe lost a little. About twilight, I walked into a clump of bushes and vines on the bank of the lake in Central Park. I injected over two grains in the flesh of my thigh and, fearful that it would not be sufficient, swallowed the remaining two grains. It was with the calmest, happiest feeling that I felt unconsciousness stealing over me. I woke up alive to my utter disgust, after several hours' unconsciousness."

Here the writer devotes two closely written pages to remarks on the curse of intemperance. He declares that he is a Spiritualist who has drank of the waters of philosophy and adds: "In dying, as I do, I know that I am acting contrary to all the teachings of this philosophy, but I am very weary and death is enticing. I hope I will be more successful in winning her regard this time. I think my mind is well-balanced and I have no fear of death. What little fear I did possess has been dissipated by the facts of Spiritualism. The mere act of dying is nothing to me, if there is not physical pain, and I think I know somewhat of the country to which I am going.

Well, bye bye old world, I believe I have enough of you!"

New York Times
September 7th, 1881

MAGNETISM

And

SOMNAMBULISM

or Simply and Solely

MOUNTEBANKISM

The force and process harnessed by the German doctor, Franz Mesmer, was known by many names: Mesmerism, Animal Magnetism, Hypnotism, Electro-Biology, Zoism ... And, with each name and practitioner, came a different way of working and many different imagined customs.

Many of these practitioners passed through Dublin, offering miraculous cures and supernatural perception, but one of the study's strangest proponents was already well-known as a lawyer and professor in Trinity College.

Which 'ism' it is that predominates,
Whether magnetism and somnambulism,
Or, simply and solely, mountebankism.

From *Animal Magnetism*
Sir Thomas Moore
1838

ON MESMERISM

A universal medicine composed of art seems an absurdity; but the transfusion of the *vis medicatrix naturae* from one system to another, granting it to be possible, would, of necessity, accomplish the results so foolishly anticipated from merely chemical compounds. If, in mesmeric experiments, we have to do with the vital force itself, then have we mastered the desideratum of ages and stand on the vestibule of that temple whose adyta will yet unveil to us the majestic realities of primeval knowledge. Mesmerism, as a medical application, transcends the limits of authentic history, and looms out from amidst the shadows of remote antiquity, as the mighty heritage of sacerdotal castes and the priceless attainment of long-sought and successful initiation into the secrets of a wisdom that was already old when Greece was in the first dawn of her advancing knowledge and the 'seven hills' were a hunting-ground for Italy's untutored aborigines.

Lectures on Mesmerism, delivered at the Rotunda, Dublin
J.W. Jackson
Published 1835

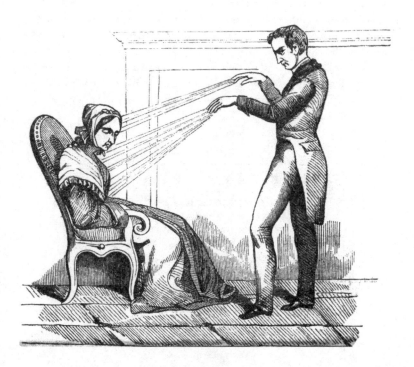

Mechanics' INSTITUTION
MR. G.W. STONE'S LECTURES ON ELECTRO-BIOLOGY

The lectures now in course of delivery at "the Institute" by the talented professor of mesmeric science are well-attended and an increased degree of interest seems to pervade the audience at each successive lecture with regard to the theories so boldly and, it must be said, fairly propounded by the lecturer, illustrated as they are by most startling facts and sustained by phenomena of the most interesting character. Amidst no section of our public could a professor of mesmeric science find an audience less disposed to receive theory without proof than amidst the young and intelligent society of artisans constituting the bulk of the members of the Mechanics' Institution and it would seem no weak proof of the success of Mr. Stone's experiments that his lectures continue to draw, on each stated evening, crowded and attentive audiences. In accordance with the wishes of a large section of the members, Mr Stone resumed, last evening, his experiments on individuals not previously thrown into the mesmeric coma, but in a perfectly wakeful state. The results of these experiments were, in many instances, most successful and excited the highest wonder among all present, but in none was greater surprise evinced than by those who were the casual subjects of experiment.

The next lecture to be given by Mr. Stone on this deeply interesting subject will be delivered at the Mechanics' Institute on next Saturday evening, when a series of novel illustrative experiments will be instituted. We perceive that Mr. Stone proposes to receive a class for instruction in electric-biology and intends to induct his pupils into the method of conducting experiments for their own amusement and instruction.

Freeman's Journal
March 18th, 1852

Electro   BIOLOGY
LAST NIGHT BUT ONE
Mr. G.W. STONE'S Wonderful Experiments at
THE MECHANICS' INSTITUTE
On THIS EVENING (Saturday), 20th March.
Body of the Hall, 1s; Gallery 6d.
And positively for the last time in Dublin, on Monday Evening, March 22nd, on which occasion all who attend will learn how to experiment.

Admission, 2s. No Free List except to those having Mr. Stone's Work, just published by Mr. McGlashan, 30, Upper Sackville-street Doors open at Eight; to commence at Half-past Eight.

```
┌─────────────────────────────────────────────────────────┐
│  R    O    T    U    N    D    O                          │
│             Entrance Under the Clock                      │
│         ELECTRO BIOLOGY AND PHRENOLOGY                    │
│                 PROFESSOR STONE                           │
│  Begs to announce that in consequence of the great success│
│  which has attended his                                   │
│             EXPERIMENTS IN ELECTRO-BIOLOGY,               │
│  and the unabated interest manifested by crowded and      │
│  highly respectable audiences during the past three weeks,│
│  his Entertainment will be continued EVERY EVENING THIS   │
│  WEEK, and upon each occasion a great variety of truly    │
│           WONDERFUL AND AMUSING EXPERIMENTS               │
│  will be performed upon persons in a perfectly wakeful state.│
│       Admission—First seats, 2s, Second seats, 1s.        │
│     Doors open at Half-past Seven; to commence at Eight   │
│  o'Clock.                                                 │
│     Tickets may be obtained during the day of Mr McKAY,   │
│  Rotundo, and at the door.                                │
│     P.S. —Phrenological Examinations may be obtained      │
│  daily at No. 8, Upper Sackville street, between the hours of│
│  Twelve noon and Five p.m. Terms—Verbal examinations, 3s. │
│  6d.; full Written Charts, 12s. 6d.                       │
└─────────────────────────────────────────────────────────┘
```

LECTURES ON MESMERISM

Let people say what they will, either in vehement anger or with the affectation of derisive incredulity, it is an extraordinary fact — one which at any rate they cannot affect to ignore — that for forty nights, during a period of little more than two months, forty lectures have been delivered on the subject in Dublin, elucidated by the most curious and singular phenomena of the science (if the term be not premature). Doubtless the great ability, the extensive knowledge, and the admirable command of language evinced by the lecturer, Mr. Jackson, and the honest, successful, and decidedly earnest experiments of Mr. Davey must have done much towards the popularity of these lectures; but to be able to command crowded audiences for such a length of time is an evidence that the influence of the faculty in this regard and in Dublin is gone. We remember that, a few years ago, M. La Fontaine (and he was doubtless a clever man) would be hardly listened to. There were rows almost every evening gotten up by some surgeon's or apothecary's apprentice or by some smart shopman who had no other way of distinguishing himself in public. The doctors laughed and joked and the Frenchman was ultimately obliged to beat a retreat. How different has it been at present, it is superfluous to say; and, although there have been some occasional interruptions, we confess we are very agreeably surprised to learn that they have been so few. Nay, we learn that there has been a bray from a fanatical or roguish parson, sorely in want of a topic, against mesmerism (clergymen of the establishment in England being the most unexceptionable witnesses of mesmeric facts). These have produced no effect upon the public. We have not visited the Rotunda more than twice, owing principally to the distance of our residence in the country from the Rotunda and from the indisposition natural to elderly persons to stir from home after dinner: but we saw enough of the remarkable talent of the lecturer and the zeal and mastery of his art in the experimenter to satisfy ourselves of their knowledge and integrity. As to the matter itself, we require neither the testimony of our sense nor the light of reasoning.

Dublin Evening Post
June 17th, 1850

EFFECTS OF MESMERISM

J. C. M'Kewen, a member of the Society of Friends, stated on the public platform, that he had been mesmerized by Mr. Davey for medical purposes and increased seven pounds in weight in three weeks, while subjected to his treatment.

Dublin Commercial Journal
March 15th, 1852

ON SLEEP

The sweet slumbers of childhood can be commanded at pleasure and the wait of its young nature, under the sufferings to which it is so frequently exposed, may be exchanged for the profound placidity of a dreamless sleep, without the administration of one nauseous or noxious ingredient. Whenever it is thought that a simple recipe might be safely administered without the formality of medical advice, there, at least, mesmerism may be tried, even by the simplest individual, with safety and advantage. Let us not, then, neglect the due culture of a dawning power which promises to endow the parent, the friend, the clergyman, and the philanthropist with an exhaustless treasury, whose priceless gift of health is one which the wealth of princes has but too often failed to purchase.

Lectures on Mesmerism, delivered at the Rotunda, Dublin
J.W. Jackson
Published 1835

MESMERISM AND SURGICAL OPERATIONS

Operations during Sham Sleep – With respect to the fact of a person submitting without moan or effort to have his teeth drawn, everyone knows that some persons, be the cause what it may, suffer less pain from the process or have nerve to bear it better than others. We see the same in all surgical operations. The other day a young woman had the operation of tracheotomy performed on her by Mr Orr, in the City of Dublin Hospital, and, during the entire operation, not a moan audible to the lookers-on escaped her nor a struggle requiring the slight restraint was made by her. Now, had this girl been subjected to the manipulations of a mesmeric juggler or had the medical men present been such simpletons as to co-operate with the promoters of these delusions, we should never have had an end of the rejoicings for such a crowning triumph of mesmerism.

Dublin Medical Press
1845

MR. DE LESSART,

HAVING brought his COMPOSITION TEETH to a degree of perfection beyond what his expectations could have anticipated and having received from such Ladies and Gentlemen as have made use of them the warmest approbation and acknowledgements, feels confident that a trial is all that is required to convince the public of their superior claims to their attention. It is impossible but the use of HUMAN TEETH must be accompanied with many disagreeable sensations; the wearer of the Composition is not only free from any unpleasantness of this kind, but also has the satisfaction of experiencing that time makes no alteration in the appearance and texture of the Teeth, whereas the HUMAN TEETH and, indeed, all ANIMAL MATTER must soon lose their colour and become offensive to the wearer. So exact an imitation is this Composition of the most beautiful enamel of the best Teeth, in their most perfect state, that none who have not seen them could possibly believe it.

TOOTH EXTRACTION UNDER LOCAL MESMERISM

DENTISTRY

In the summer of 1851, while lecturing in Dublin, Mr. Welsh, a young gentleman of that city, "who wished to have the stumps of two teeth extracted, expressed his desire that it should be effected while he was under mesmeric influence; and Mr. Davey, finding that he had considerable power over him, thought that local insensibility might be induced and prove amply sufficient for the intended object. With this view, he made the requisite passes over the jaw, and the extraction was accordingly performed without producing the least uneasiness, although the patient remained awake during the operation, which must have been rather severe, as a part of the inferior maxillary* was brought away.

18, Great Longford Street, Dublin,
Nov. 19, 1851.

'For several months I was labouring under disease of the chest and lungs. I sought medical advice, but got no relief. I went to Mr. Davey and got relief on the third sitting, which increased on each visit until I was perfectly cured.

William Harrison.

The Illustrated Practical Mesmerist: Curative and Scientific
William Davey
3rd Edition, 1861

---

*   The jawbone.

FORWARDED TO THE EDITOR BY MR. DAVEY
TO MESSRS DAVEY AND JACKSON,
7, Upper Sackville Street.

Merton, Cullenswood, Dublin,
March 21, 1851

Dear Sir, Since I had the pleasure of attending your interesting lecture last night, a fact has taken place, which I think but right to inform you of and which, no doubt, may be valuable to you to know. You may have observed that my son had an abscess on his left temple and which this morning was much enlarged and EXCEEDINGLY PAINFUL when the medical man saw it and examined it; he said it would be necessary to open it. The boy was adverse to this; but I said, Come I will put you to sleep and you shall not feel it. I, accordingly, in the presence of several persons, in less than four minutes, had him in what you call a "comfortable sleep." The doctor asked was he ready: I said yes; when he opened it, making rather a deep cut, from which there was an immense discharge. The boy never flinched or moved in the SLIGHTEST DEGREE. I then made some upward passes, when he immediately awakened and enquired directly, was it yet done? I replied in the affirmative, but he would scarcely believe it until he saw the discharge from it, declaring he DID NOT FEEL IT IN THE SLIGHTEST DEGREE. Thus giving one more proof of the practical uses mesmerism may be applied to: and, I assure you, I feel greatly obliged to you for having opened my eyes to see its value and truth, as when properly applied, it cannot but be a boon to poor suffering humanity. The medical gentleman that opened the abscess was Mr. William Waters. You have my full permission to make what private use you please of this statement.

I am, dear Sirs, yours truly,
Falconer Miles.

Published in The *Zoist*
October 1851

Richard Whately (1787–1863) was the Church of Ireland Archbishop of Dublin. He was a noted logician, economist, and eccentric, and imagined himself an authority on science and theology. As a public proponent of phrenology and mesmerism, he failed to be either. After a week-long course of mesmerism, he was cured of rheumatism.

GOUT.

MESMERIC ASSOCIATION

Another Mesmeric Institute was established in Dublin*, in the year 1852, under the patronage of His Grace the Archbishop of Dublin, of which Falconer Miles was president. The following prospectus clearly sets forth its objects and the principles adopted for its guidance. It is typical of all the institutions named in this connection in utterly repudiating the superstitious assumptions of supernaturalism and placing the practice upon a purely scientific basis:

The Committee of the Dublin Mesmeric Association, in appealing to their fellow-citizens on behalf of a Mesmeric Hospital, feel themselves called on to explain the character and objects of the Association and to remove some misconceptions which prevail, or might be likely to arise, on the subject. They wish it to be distinctly understood that their object is not to maintain or to devise any scientific theory, but simply to extend the knowledge of certain important facts and to facilitate the beneficial application of that knowledge in the relief of suffering and the cure of disease.

The Committee beg also to be understood, most clearly and candidly, that they do not seek to produce Mesmerism before the public as an agent

---

* The Association conducted its first meetings at 13, Anglesea Street.

capable of curing all diseases or by any means wish it to usurp the place of the medical man; but simply put it forward as an individual remedy, capable of controlling and exercising a powerful and beneficial influence over a vast number of ailments; and more especially those called nervous and chronic affections, which medical men have at all times acknowledged as little benefited by the mere administration of drugs.

RHEUMATISM

The Committee feel it of vital importance to their own character, to the people, and to the cause of Mesmerism itself, to disclaim any connection or co-operation with those who receive or practice Mesmerism, as derived from supernatural agency or miracle-working power independent of the laws of creation; but, on the contrary, would more humbly and gratefully acknowledge it as an additional means granted by the Almighty to man, to make him more dependent on Him and more useful to his fellow-man; and believe its phenomena to be solely the result of the vital force, conveyed by the operator to the more delicate and susceptible nervous organization of the person mesmerized; just as light or heat or sound, &c., variously affect the animal or organic tissues they come in contact with.

Lastly, the Committee would suggest to the public and in particular to the medical men of this city that, when the existence of a real and important agent has been established by facts, which it is vain to attempt denying, and, when great and increasing public attention has been drawn to these facts, it is most important to the well-being of society that such an agent should not be left in the hands of the ignorant and thoughtless or of designing or ill-disposed persons; but that means should be taken for affording all candid persons an opportunity of fair investigation; so that truth may be distinguished from falsehood and a beneficial from a noxious or dangerous application of the powers which Providence has placed within our reach."

By Order.

J. MacDonnell,

Hon. Secretary.

Vital Magnetism: Its Power Over Disease
Frederick T. Parson
1877

SUCCESSFUL CURES ENACTED BY THE MESMERIC SOCIETY, AS CLAIMED BY IVER MCDONNELL, HON. SEC., IN A LETTER TO THE FREEMAN'S JOURNAL, NOVEMBER 13TH, 1852.

James Ryan	Labourer	Ball's-bridge	Rheumatic pains	Cured in three sittings
James Doyle	Bricklayer	4 Longford-lane	Partial paralysis of the left side, accompanied by occasional mental derangement	Cured in four sittings
Edward B.	4-year-old child	Sandford-terrace	Deafness	Cured in two sittings
George Haughton	House painter	Temple-bar	Rheumatic pains	Cured in five sittings
Thomas Toony	8-year-old child	Tennis-court	Deafness	Cured in thirty sittings

INSTRUCTION FROM MR. CHENEVIX

About 1828, Mr. Richard Chenevix visited Dublin for the purpose of giving demonstrations in mesmerism. He visited Steevens' Hospital for this purpose and Mr. J.W. Cusack directed Mr. Cullinan, his apprentice, to select from amongst the pupils some eligible subjects for the demonstrations. This being done, about eight students – including the late Charles Lever, the novelist, who at the time was a resident pupil in the hospital – assembled in Mr. Cullinan's room to witness the performance. Mr. Chevenix requested that the number of spectators should be reduced to two, in order to maintain that quietness which was an essential element in the success of his performances. Mr. Cullinan requested the withdrawal of those whose attendance at a lecture about to be delivered was not necessary, in order that those who were required to attend it should first have the opportunity of witnessing the performance. Mr. Smith refused to leave, and an unpleasant altercation having ensued, Mr. Cullinan requested Mr. Smith to go out into the corridor with him. Mr. Cullinan, under the influence of strong emotion, became very pale, which being noticed by Mr. Smith, he exclaimed loudly – "How pale the cowardly fellow is." Mr. Cullinan thereupon struck him with his open hand upon his face, saying – "That is the only answer I can give your observation." In a few minutes the hospital porter brought Mr. Cullinan a note from Mr. Smith, challenging him to a hostile meeting. Charles Lever was successively solicited by both belligerents to act as a second, but declined. At this time Mr. Cullinan was a Scholar of T.C.D. and, as the statutes of the College provided for the expulsion of students who fought duels, he was anxious to keep the Board of T.C.D. in ignorance of the intended rencontre. Meeting Mr. Smith on his way to a lecture, he stopped and requested him not to mention the proposed duel in such a way that the Board might obtain cognisance of it, whereupon Mr. Smith said that he was a very impertinent fellow to address him. Next morning at six o'clock the "affair" came off in the Phoenix Park; Capt. Cruikshank acting as "second" to Mr. Smith and Capt. Beatty said that he was not, as his principal had been insulted by Mr. Smith. Ultimately hostilities terminated on Mr. Smith expressing regret for having insulted Mr. Cullinan, and apologising for his conduct.

History of the Royal College of Surgeons in Ireland
Charles Cameron
1916

CLAIRVOYANCE

Prior to concluding this department of the subject, it may be as well to make a few remarks on the much debated question of clairvoyance. That, as a fact in nature, this condition of supersensuous exaltation does really exist cannot for a moment be seriously doubted by anyone thoroughly acquainted with mesmerism, either by experimental or documentary evidence. It is, however, much rarer than is usually supposed. Under it, the subject is capable of exercising perception, under conditions that, in his ordinary state, would render it impossible. He may prove capable of prevision, postvision, distant vision, and thought-reading and, thus, afford revelations apparently incredible to those ignorant of the additional capability with which, while in this state, he seems to be endowed. The achievements of a good "lucid" are such as to show that all the phenomena connected with the American spirit-rapping may be accounted for without having recourse to the theory of supernatural agency.

The subject, whose initials are here given, is a gentleman of good family, then a student of Trinity College, Dublin, and now in holy orders. At his request his name is not given; but those of the authenticating witnesses are sufficient, it is hoped, to prove the genuineness of the document.

7, Upper Sackville Street,
8th July, 1851.

We, the undersigned, having been present when Mr. H. W. B., T. C. D., divinity student of the senior class, resident at Richmond Street, Mountjoy Square, was placed in the mesmeric trance by Mr. Davey, at his rooms, 7, Upper Sackville Street. We determined fully to test the truth of the experiment, taking care to convince ourselves that it was utterly impossible for him to have seen objects by his natural vision — his eyes having been closed and covered by the hands of several of us — do hereby certify, that he read passages and words in various books, of which he had no previous knowledge; and, from the manner of his describing various objects as they moved about or were placed in the room, are fully convinced of the truthfulness of the experiment, which was entirely satisfactory and conclusive to all present, several of whom are utter strangers to Mr. B.

R.B. Alexander, 19, Richmond Place.
J.C. Hayes, 22, Portland Row.
Augustus Johnston, A.B., T.C.D., 9 Upper Pembroke Street.
Guy Crawford, 1, North Cumberland St.
T.W. Poole, Whitworth Place.

7, Upper Sackville Street,
9th July, 1851.

Having again met to witness a repetition of the experiments yesterday made on Mr. H. W. B., we observed similar results, and the impression produced on our minds was a positive conviction as to the truth of clairvoyance, to which we desire to record our testimony. Mr. B.'s eyes were held down by a gentleman present while he read papers as they were presented to him.

T.W. Poole; E.B. Alexander; K.H. Blake Butler;
Junr. Guy Crawford; Augustus Johnston.

I was present on the 9th of July and saw Mr. B.'s clairvoyant reading – of the truth of which I am convinced.

Henry O'Neill,
Anglesea Buildings.

The Illustrated Practical Mesmerist: Curative and Scientific
William Davey
3rd Edition, 1861

Hill Hamilton Hardy was many things: a barrister at law; a Trinity College Dublin mathematician; an author, clairvoyant, prophet, and healer. That he was something of a sham makes all these achievements the more impressive. Becoming widely known in Dublin as a mesmerist, he sat down to the task of writing the book on Spirit Magnetism. It took him a fortnight alone to reach the end of the title.

THIS DAY PUBLISHED, Price **2s. 6d.**,

ANALYTIC RESEARCHES IN SPIRIT MAGNETISM,

considered as the Key to the Mysteries of Nature and Revelation, and the Medium of Communication with the Invisible Worlds; all tending to indicate the Importance of

E C S T A C Y and **C L A I R V O Y A N C E**,

and the Psychological Phenomena of

ELECTRO - BIOLOGY

By Hill H. Hardy, A.M., T.C.D.,

BARRISTER-AT-LAW

Author of *"Geometrical Properties of Polygons."*
Dublin: GEORGE MASON, 24, D'Oiler-street.

AN INTRODUCTION

I have been requested to publish all my letters that have appeared in the Dublin papers; from the beginning of the contest with the Medical Profession to its close, together with those in which I announced my discoveries in clairvoyance and my experiments with the magic mirror, &c. This I shall do as soon as possible, giving in full the revelations respecting Sir John Franklin that I was obliged to curtail from want of space. The sequel of this work will, I trust, be ready as soon as the public are prepared to receive it, with all the revelations of my ecstatics; but I am quite aware that, in the present, I have given out more food for reflection than will be digested for some time. I shall continue from this forward to publish any important and well-attested cases of clairvoyance that may present themselves.

In conclusion, I may state that, as my chief task is done, I am now ready to apply Mesmerism, Phreno-Mesmerism, and Electro-Biology, to the cure of disease. In the sequel of this work, the reader will find a list of cures in which I have already succeeded, in one of which the patient was given up by several of the Medical Profession and is now in perfect health. And now I must close for the present and it remains for my readers to decide when I shall next address them and whether in person or spirit.

Hill Hamilton Hardy, A.M., T.C.D.
10 D'Olier Street, Dublin
March 5th, 1852
From *Analytic Researches in Spirit-Magnetism*

No such sequel was forthcoming, but Hamilton continued to perform and tour extensively, seemingly able to take plenty of time away from his legal and mathematical duties.

Mesmerism-Illustrated Lectures
BY HILL H. HARDY, A.M., T.C.D.

Considerable interest having been excited amongst certain intellectual circles in our city with regard to some recent novel and startling effects resulting from the exercise of mesmeric agency as administered by Mr. Hardy, a numerous assemblage of ladies and gentry attended on yesterday at that gentleman's chambers in D'Olier-street, at one o'clock, for the purpose of witnessing a series of experiments illustrative of the alleged extraordinary efficacy of the mesmeric power in the case of epileptic and other diseases of the character usually termed "nervous" and also with the view of satisfying themselves as to the credibility of some extraordinary phenomena recently presented in clairvoyant subjects. He introduced to the assemblage a young man, seemingly of about twenty years of age, who, it appeared, had been since his childhood a martyr to epileptic fits.

Mr. Hardy proceeded to place his patient in the rigid state, during the continuance of which his arms were kept horizontally extended for a considerable time. Having been released from the rigid state and from the state of coma, the patient was then subjected, by Mr. Hardy, to the influence of the operator's will, whilst in the waking state, and the results, so far as could be judged from obvious appearance, were conclusive as to the desperate command exercised by the mesmerist over the physical and even mental energies of the patient. When told that the temperature of the room was freezing, the patient exhibited involuntary indications of chilliness and, when told that the floor beneath his feet was inappropriately hot, he shifted his position and perspiration stood in drops on his forehead. He was fixed to the floor and allowed to move apparently at the will of the operator; but, on Mr. Hardy assuring the patient that he was dumb, the native spirit of contradiction got too strong for mesmeric credence and the patient also refused to surrender his memory at the bidding of the operator. It was stated that a considerable period had elapsed since the young man had experienced a return of his illness.

Freeman's Journal
March 20th, 1852

Mr. Hardy travelled as far as Australia and New Zealand to present the benefits of Spirit-Magnetism. This he did mostly by encouraging blindfolded volunteers to identify objects chosen at random by the audience. The answer was generally a watch.

MESMERISM

It may be in the recollection of our readers that Sir Philip Crampton, some time since, in order to test the powers alleged to be possessed by persons in what is called the clairvoyant state produced by the mysterious influence of mesmerism, offered to enclose a bank note for £100 in a sealed envelope, which should become the property of any individual who could, while blindfolded and in the mesmeric sleep, tell its date and number. The challenge has been accepted by Mr. Hill H. Hardy.

London Lancet
January 1852

IN CONCLUSION

We are greater than we know, sons of the Infinite; we inherit a germ, whose roots may yet be nourished in the soil of Time and Space, but whose blossoms already prepare to extend their fragrance through the shadeless vistas of an ever-present Here and an everlasting Now.

Lectures on Mesmerism, delivered at the Rotunda, Dublin
J.W. Jackson
Published 1835

The Magnetic Girl
How She Compels Others To Obey Her Will.

100,000 Copies of Remarkable Book describing peculiar Psychic Powers to be distributed Post Free to readers of Dublin "Irish Times."

"The wonderful power of Personal Influence, Magnetism, Fascination, Mind Control, call it what you will, can surely be acquired by everyone, no matter how unattractive or unsuccessful," says Mr. Elmer Ellsworth Knowles, author of the new book entitled: "The Key to the Development of the Inner Forces."

The book, which is being distributed free of charge, is full of photographic reproductions showing how these skills are being used all over the world and how thousands upon thousands have developed powers which they little dreamed they possessed.

Irish Times

WHAT IS
YET TO
COME

Dublin is an old city and Ireland an older country. There is no escaping history and no Irish person could forget it, even if they wanted to. The future looms just as darkly and the means to escape it are none too inviting. There are those who will go on about the future, as any pub drunk will go on about the past, but, if you want to enjoy the present, you won't listen to either of them.

Astronomy teaches the situation and motion of the heavenly bodies: Astrology pretends to explain their influence on human affairs. Astronomy is founded on knowledge: astrology on fancy. Astronomy belongs to the learned: astrology to the ignorant. An astrologer bears the same relations to an astronomer that a quack does to a physician.

Dublin Penny Journal
January 18th, 1834

———— **REMARKABLE PROPHECY** ————

Dublin, which has in hand a very ambitious scheme for the extension of the city boundaries, had an origin in a very remote period.

First it was Billy Ath Claith, the Town of the Ford of Hurdles; then it became Bally Ath Claith Dubb Linne, The Town of the Ford of Hurdles on the Black River, and so Dublin.

According to tradition, St. Patrick foretold great things for it. "That small village shall hereafter be an eminent city: it shall increase in eminence and dignity, until at length it shall be lifted up unto the throne of the kingdom."

The *Mail*
November 6th, 1926

PROPHETS: FRANCIS DOBBS.

Among the characters introduced to the readers of "N. & Q.," [Notes & Queries] under the name of prophets, there are few that deserve so distinguished a place as Mr. Francis Dobbs. As, however, we have to deal with Mr. Dobbs chiefly as a religious prophet, I shall confine my extracts from his speeches to the illustration of his character in that capacity.

On June 7th 1800, Mr. Dobbs pronounced, in the Irish Parliament, a speech in which he predicted the second coming of the Messiah. This speech, the most extraordinary that was ever made in a legislative assembly, presents a singular contrast to the sagacity which characterises his political performances. A few short extracts will show the change that had come over his prophetic vision:

"It was not very difficult to foresee that it should fall to your lot to pronounce the painful words, 'That this bill do pass.' * Awful indeed would

—————————————
* The Union with Ireland Act 1800.

those words be to me, did I consider myself living in ordinary times: but feeling as I do that we are not living in ordinary times — feeling as I do that we are living in the most momentous and eventful period of the world — feeling as I do that a new and better order of things is about to arise and that Ireland, in that new order of things, is to be highly distinguished indeed — this bill hath no terrors for me.

"I shall for the present confine myself to such passages as will support three positions: — The first is, the certainty of the second advent of the Messiah; the next, the signs of the times of his coming, and the manner of it; and the last, that Ireland is to have the glorious pre-eminence of being the first kingdom that will receive him."

After dwelling, at some length on his first two positions, he thus proceeds:

"I come now, Sir, to the most interesting part of what I have to say; it is to point out my reasons for thinking this is the distinguished country in which the Messiah is now to appear.

"There are some very particular circumstances attending Ireland. She has never had her share in worldly prosperity, and has only since 1782 begun to rise; and I know no instance in history of any nation beginning to prosper, without arriving at a summit of some kind, before it became again depressed. The four great empires rose progressively west of each other; and Great Britain made the last toe of the image, being the last conquest the Romans made in the west. Now, Ireland lies directly west of it, and is therefore in exactly the same progressive line, and it never was any part of the image, nor did the Roman arms ever penetrate here. The arms of Ireland is the harp of David, with an angel in its front. The crown of Ireland is the apostolic crown. Tradition has long spoken of it as a land of saints; and if what I expect happens, that prediction will be fulfilled. But what I rely on more than all is our miraculous exemption from all of the serpent and venomous tribe of reptiles. This appears to me in the highest degree emblematic, that Satan, the Great Serpent, is here to receive his first deadly blow."

Notes and Queries: A Medium of Inter-Communication
for Literary Men, Artists, Antiquaries, Genealogist, Etc.
January 28th, 1854

In June 1849, a reader named Otis wrote to the *Dublin Evening Mail* to explain his proof, via intricate calculations of 'prophetic time,' that the Prophet Daniel had predicted the escape – in disguise as a woman – of Pope Pius IX from the Quirinal Palace.* Unfortunately for those involved, this solution was provided 8 months after the event had taken place on November 24th, 1848.

---

* See Daniel 7–12

PIVS · PAPA · IX · P · M

ON ATHEISM
Dublin, 2nd May, 1809

Sir,

I was some time ago at a crowded and fashionable party. In
the group I was in, it was whispered, that a Magnetizer
was in company and the Magnetizer was prevailed on to
come into a small room to shew a specimen of the art.
She was a good-humoured lady and, after selecting her
company - a delicate, young lady - she shut the door.
The young lady was soon observed to be in a trance, which
continued till the patience of the company was exhausted.
The Magnetizer appeared much alarmed, air was admitted,
smelling bottles used, and the magnetized lady's dress

loosened, with these means animation returned, but it was still more alarming, by the appearance of convulsions, like a strong fit of the falling sickness; the wretched subject of this wicked delusion was carried up to bed and got some medicines; as she recovered she became hysterical and the Magnetizer declared she never saw so bad a case.

If you please to insert this with the enclosed letter from a physician in Hamburg and the report of a committee at Paris, on the Animal Magnetism practised by Mesmer, it may serve to warn the thoughtless about this diabolical practice, which appears to have originated in that Antichristian Empire of Atheism, France, as a mode of proving that all dreams, visions, and prophecies, are natural productions, which leads directly to the motto of Atheism, that "Every man is his own God."

The atheists of France labour to reject the Bible; they discuss the age of the world and calculate by the hardness of Volcanic Lava, that it is older than the statement in Genesis. They seek to find the site of Babylon in opposition to the prophecy that it is not to be found. They strive to controvert true prophecy in numberless points; they wish to blot the idea of another world in a future state, from the mind, holding it as the bane of unprincipled success; they are against Christ and his prophets and by the fictitious miracles of Somnambulism, Magnetism, Mechanism, Chemistry, Galvinism, Phantasmagoria, Ventriloquism, and Acoustics, they endeavour to explain everything Supernatural as a work of art.

I am, Sir, &c. &c.

Supernatural Magazine
June 1809

Aleister Crowley (1875–1947), English occultist, artist, ceremonial magician, and – most famously – Great Beast, was born in Leamington Spa to English parents, where he was given the name Edward Alexander. He was no more Irish than he was "the wickedest man in the world." However, he adopted the name of Aleister as a Gaelicised version of his own and claimed Irish heritage. By the time of this

New York stunt (see below), he had already declared himself Sovereign Grand Master General of Ireland, Iona, and all the Britons. Although it is uncertain whether Crowley ever visited Ireland.

As founder of the religion of Thelema, he pronounced himself a prophet whose visions would lead humanity into the Æon of Horus and his story is entwined with many of the important events of the first half of the twentieth century.

His attempt to prophesy, a year early, Ireland's declaration of independence may have a less mystic origin. Crowley was a double-agent for British Intelligence and the event was orchestrated to undermine American support for Dublin and Berlin during The Great War.

IRISH REPUBLIC BORN IN NEW YORK HARBOR

TEN PATRIOTS AT DAYBREAK RENOUNCE ALLEGIANCE TO ENGLAND NEAR STATUE OF LIBERTY
INDEPENDENCE IS DECLARED

As dawn was slowly spreading over the city on the morning of July 3rd, a thirty-foot launch slipped from the recreation pier at the foot of West Fiftieth Street and glided down the Hudson. On board were ten persons, silent and serious with the consciousness of what was to

Samara Leibner

them a profoundly solemn and significant ceremony.

In the prow of the boat was Aleister Crowley, Irishman-poet, philosopher, explorer, a man of mystic mind – the leader of an Irish hope. Of nearly middle age and mild in manner, with the intellectual point of view colored with cabalistic interpretation, Crowley is an unusual man, capably so to those who believe and feel in common with him. He is said to be a close friend of William Butler Yeats,[*] the

---

[*] Crowley and Yeats were far from friends. After the formation of the Hermetic Society Dublin, the Nobel Laureate went on to join the Hermetic Order of the Golden Dawn, of which Crowley was also a member. The two ultimately vied for leadership of the order, a contest that came to a head when they confronted each other at the headquarters on Blythe Road, Kensington, on April 19th 1900.

To continue the confusion over his nationality, Crowley arrived in full Highland dress, wearing a mask of Osiris, and carrying a gilt dagger. Yeats brought a professional boxer for company and, when Crowley was discovered attempting to steal the Order's secret rituals, the pair had to remove The Great Ape by force. The poet won the resulting court case.

Crowley was on slightly better terms with Oscar Wilde, as it was he who unveiled Jacob Epstein's statue for the playwright's monument in 1914. It was also Crowley who removed the bronze butterfly that Paris officials affixed to obscure the figure's genitals.

Irish poet, and he has written several Irish poems himself.

READY TO WAR ON ENGLAND

The early morning mission of July 3rd was to declare the independence of the Irish Republic, which included a declaration of war against England, and to pledge their allegiance to the government of their vision.

The leader of the party, Crowley, in whose mysticism there is something of astrology, had read the heavens and found that the conjunction of certain stars was auspicious for Ireland at exactly 4:32 o'clock on the morning of July 3rd.

So, with the launch a few feet off Bedloe's Island, at the moment of 4:32 o'clock, Crowley rose to begin the ceremony. He said:

"I have not asked any great human audience to listen to these words; I had rather address them to the unconquerable ocean that surrounds the world, and to the free four winds of heaven. Facing the sunrise, I lift up my hands and my soul herewith to this giant figure of Liberty, the ethical counterpart of the Light, Life, and Love which are our spiritual heritage. In this symbolical and most awful act of religion I invoke the one true God of whom the sun himself is but a shadow that he may strengthen me in heart and hand to uphold that freedom for the land of my sires, which I am come hither to proclaim.

"I unfurl the Irish flag. I proclaim the Irish Republic. Erin go Bragh. God save Ireland."

As the bits of the torn English passport scattered over the surface of the water the Irish flag, a green field supporting a golden harp, flapped free in the breeze from a mast in the bow of the boat.

New York Times
July 13th, 1915

CHEIRO: PALM-READER TO THE STARS
Count Hamon, who practices as a palmist under the title of "Cheiro," was cross-examined as to his profession and practice.

Mr. Macarkie – What is palmistry?

If we went into a discussion upon that I am afraid it would take up a great deal of your time and too much of mine.

Mr. Macarkie – Does palmistry profess from the lines of the hand to read the character or does it profess to foretell the future?

It tells the character and temperament from the lines of the hand

Does it not profess to tell the future?

You may profess that.

Do you profess to tell that?

I may tell very closely indeed what a person may do, being of a particular disposition or character. If a man has criminal tendencies we naturally expect he will commit criminal actions.

Freeman's Journal
June 16th, 1899

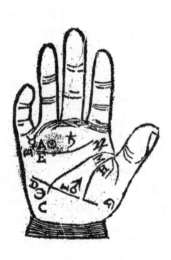

The BOOK of

PALMESTRY
AND
PHYSIOGNOMY.

BEING

Brief *introductions*, both Natural, Pleasant, and delectable, unto the Art of *Chiromancy*, or *Manual Divination*, and *Physiognomy* ; with circumstances upon the Faces of the SIGNS.

Alſo, Canons of Rules, upon *Diſeaſes* or *Sickneſſes*.

Whereunto is alſo annexed,

As well the Artificial as Natural

ASTROLOGY,

With the Nature of the PLANETS.

Written in Latine by John Indagine *Prieſt, and Tranſlated into Engliſh by* Fabian Withers.

The Seventh Edition Correĉted.

London, Printed by *J. R.* for *T. Paſſinger*, at the Bible on *London-Bridge*.

By some accounts, **William John Warner** (1866–1936) was born in a "small village outside Dublin" and, in others, by the sea at Bray. The exact coordinates would be necessary if one were to chart an accurate horoscope of the man. However, as an astrologer, numerologist and palm-reader, Warner was more interested in mystery, charm and showmanship. That is why he prefers you to call him Count Louis Hamon or, indeed, Cheiro – a name with its roots in chirology, the science of reading palms.

With greater facility than most palmists, he seemed able to prognosticate as well: he knew the future like the palm of your hand. He predicted the sinking of the *Titanic*, the death of Lord Kitchener and the abdication of Edward VIII. So skilled was he that he seemed unable to avoid stars and statesmen. At the start of his career, arriving in Liverpool from Holyhead, he had touched history before even leaving the station.

"WHAT DOES IT MEAN?"
AN EXTRACT FROM CHEIRO'S MEMOIRS

The only other occupant of the carriage was a gentleman who sat opposite with his back to the engine and had wrapped round his shoulders a heavy rug that almost concealed his face.

I can even now see those slender, intellectual-looking hands that this stranger laid before me, and how they interested me, line after line clearly marked, full of character, and of events created by character. I started by the Line of Mentality. I showed him its superior length to those of some of the designs in my book and explained to him that it denoted his power of will, of organisation, and of command over people. Then I called his attention to a well-marked Line of Destiny that was strongly traced through his hand until a little past the centre of the palm and I explained that it indicated strong individuality, a career that must play a marked role in life – a destiny, in fact, that would cause him to stand out as a leader above the common herd of humanity.

"But at the end," he said almost nervously. "What does that line show by fading out – what does it mean?"

I laughed as I said it, for I could hardly believe and I felt sure he would not, in spite of his interest. "Oh," I said, "the stopping of that sign simply means rest for you; another Napoleon sent to St. Helena, I suppose."

"But why?" he said rather excitedly. "What shall be my Waterloo?"

"A woman, without a doubt," I replied. "You see yourself how the Line of Heart breaks the Line of Destiny just below that point where it fades out." Taking his hand away, the stranger laughed – a low, quiet laugh –the laugh of a man who was sure of himself.

Shortly afterwards the train rushed into Euston and as we got our valises and sticks ready he said:

"It's strange, but that science of yours has been curiously accurate about some things – except about the woman part. There is my card; you will see

now how in some things it tallies – but the woman, no – a man with my life
has no time for women." And with a cheery "Goodbye" he jumped out,
hailed a hansom, and was off.

Looking down at the card, I read, "Charles Stewart Parnell."

Cheiro's Memoirs: The Reminiscences of a Society Palmist
William John Warner
1912

Cheiro led an illustrious career: he solved a mysterious murder by reading the
bloody handprint left behind by the murderer; survived an assassination attempt;
and toured the world. He held the hands of Sarah Bernhardt and William
Gladstone, and Mark Twain praised him for his 'humiliating accuracy'.

However, in a very full life, he considered the most touching moment to be
a meeting with Oscar Wilde in 1893. It was, perhaps, Wilde who was the more
touched by the encounter, since it inspired 'Lord Arthur Savile's Crime'.

THE RECOGNITION SCENE

The greatest hit I made that evening was in the case of Oscar Wilde. I
was however so struck with the difference in the markings of the left
and right hands, that from behind my curtain I explained that the left always
denoted the hereditary tendencies, while the right showed the developed
or attained characteristics and that when we use the left side of the brain
the nerves cross and go to the right hand, so that the right consequently
shows the true nature and development of the individual. I pointed this case
out as an example where the left had promised the most unusual destiny
of brilliancy and uninterrupted success, which was completely broken and
ruined at a certain date in the right. Almost forgetting myself for a moment,
I summed up all by saying, "the left hand is the hand of a king, but the right
that of a king who will send himself into exile."

I never met him again until I had wandered half round the world and
reached Paris in 1900. It was a lovely summer evening in the Exhibition. I
had been dining there with friends and as we sat on the terrace of one of the
principal restaurants, a strange, gaunt, broken figure passed and took a seat
far away from the crowd.

I should not have recognised him if some of our party had not exclaimed,
"Why, that's Oscar Wilde!"

"My dear friend," he said, "how good of you! Everyone cuts me now.
How good of you to come to me!"

It was no use offering him comfort or hope – his brain was too great to feed on dreams – it was awake to the terrible reality of life, to the cruel truth that Fate for him was broken.

"Your presence brought the dead past out of its grave. You remember that night at Blanche's – the very night on which I had made one of my great triumphs and you remember what you told me. How often I have thought of it since and while I picked oakum I often looked at my hands and wondered at that break so clearly shown in the mark of Fate and also wondered why I was unable to take the warning.

"You have done me good to-night. You have brought me back to myself. Now let me walk home alone through the quiet streets. We shall surely meet again in this great village of Paris."

We never met again, but I was one of the few who followed his coffin to the grave a few months later.

Cheiro's Memoirs: The Reminiscences of a Society Palmist
William John Warner
1912

THE FORTUNE-TELLING LOVE-BIRDS

Paddy was often seen as an organ-grinder; he played in Henry Street, which would not be tolerated now. The organ was provided with a cage containing two "love-birds" and a drawer containing "fortunes" printed upon small cards and, as Paddy played, he invited the passing girls to "try their fortunes." His towering figure generally drew more laughs than pence, but many girls did part with the necessary fee, whereupon Paddy would address a few words to one of the birds, which would pick out a "fortune" from the drawer with its bill.

The last time I ever saw Paddy he was selling *Old Moore's Almanac*, and loudly informing the world "things are predicted by Old Moore."

Dublin Historical Record
December 1939

DEATH OF A FORTUNE-TELLER

Yesterday, Dr. Kirwan, one of the city coroners, held an inquest on the body of Anne Griffith, aged 51 years, in her lodgings, 24, Chancery-lane. Ellen Cane stated that she lived in the same room with deceased and had known her for the last three months; "she was a regular fortune-teller by trade;" deceased's family consisted of one son and she had no other mode of life but that of a fortune-teller; the son was solely dependent on his mother's earnings in that way; on Saturday evening last witness saw her alive; she was then breathing very heavily; her son was reading a newspaper at the time and they appeared on the best of terms; he seemed very attentive to her; she used to drink very hard – in fact that was the first thing she did in the mornings; at two o'clock on Sunday morning the son called on witness to go see his mother, as he feared she was then dying; she went soon after and found her in his arms, on the bed, evidently in a dying state; she expired soon after; on that very morning a well-dressed female, between 30 and 40 years of age, came there to have her fortune told and, on being informed that she had come too late, that Mrs. Griffith was no more, she went away bitterly lamenting her disappointment and that she had not applied sooner. If only there was some way she could have known.

The jury found a verdict that Anne Griffith's death arose from dropsical effusion on her chest, the result of long continued habits of dissipation.

Freeman's Journal
October 26th, 1852

A HOAX ABROAD

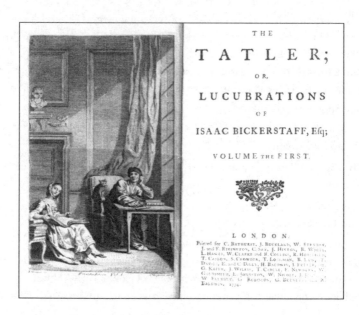

PREDICTIONS
FOR THE
YEAR 1708.

Wherein the Month and Day of the
Month are set down, the Persons
named, and the great Actions and
Events of next Year particularly
related, as they will come to pass.

Written to prevent the People of England
from being further impos'd on by
vulgar Almanack-makers.

By *ISAAC BICKERSTAFF* Esq;
MDCCVIII.

A SELECTION OF ISAAC BICKERSTAFF PREDICTIONS FOR THE YEAR 1708

April 15th – A violent Storm on the South-East Coast of France, which will destroy many of their Ships, and some in the very Harbour.

May 9th – A Mareschal of France will break his Leg by a Fall from his Horse. I have not been able to discover whether he will then dye or not.

May 15th – News will arrive of a very Surprizing Event, than which nothing could be more unexpected.

May 23rd – A famous Buffoon of the Play-house will dye of a ridiculous Death suitable to his Vocation.

June 10th – A great Battle will be fought which will begin at Four of the Clock in the Afternoon, and last till 9 at Night with great Obstinacy, but no very decisive Event.

July 12th – A Great Commander will dye a Prisoner in the Hands of his Enemies.

September 11th – The Pope having long languish'd last Month the Swellings in his Legs Breaking and the Flesh Mortifying will dye.

My first Prediction is but a Trifle, yet I will mention it, to shew how Ignorant these Sorrish Pretenders to Astrology are in their own Concerns: It relates to Partridge the Almanack-maker; I have consulted the Star of his Nativity by my own Rules, and find he will infallibly dye upon the 29th of

March next, about Eleven at night, of a raging Feaver; therefore I advise him to consider of it, and settle his Affairs in time.

Isaac Bickerstaff
1708

THE ACCOMPLISHMENT

Of the First of
Mr. Bickerstaff's Predictions.
Being an

ACCOUNT

Of the Death of
MR. PARTRIGE,
the Almanack-maker,

Upon the 29th Instant.

IN A LETTER TO A PERSON OF HONOUR WRITTEN IN THE YEAR 1708

My Lord, in Obedience to your Lordship's Commands, as well as to satisfie may own Curiosity, I have for some Days past enquired constantly after Partrige, the Almanack-maker. I saw him accidentally once or twice about 10 Days before he died, and observed he began very much to Droop and Languish, tho' I hear his Friends did not seem to apprehend him in any Danger. About Two or Three Days ago he grew Ill, was confin'd first to his Chamber, and in a few Hours after to his Bed, where Dr. Gase and Mrs. Kirlens were sent for to Visit and to Prescribe to him. Upon this Intelligence I sent thrice every Day one Servant or other to enquire after his Health; and yesterday, about Four in the Afternoon, Word was brought me that he was past Hopes.

A true and impartial account of the proceedings of Isaac Bickerstaff, Esq; against me——

The 28th of March, Anno Dom. 1708, being the night this sham-prophet had so impudently fix'd for my last, which made little impression on myself; but I cannot answer for my whole family; for my wife, with a concern more than usual, prevailed on me to take somewhat to sweat for a cold; and, between the hours of eight and nine, to go to bed: The maid, as she was warming my bed, with a curiosity natural to young wenches, runs to the window, and asks of one passing the street, who the bell toll'd for? Dr. Partridge, says he, that famous almanack-maker, who died suddenly this evening.

My wife at this fell into a violent disorder; and I must own I was a little discomposed at the oddness of the accident. In the mean time, one knocks at my door. As soon as I could compose myself, I went to him. "Sir," says I, "my name is Partridge."

"Oh! the Doctor's brother, belike," cries he, "The Doctor must needs die rich, he had great dealings in his way for many years."

With that, I assumed a great air of authority and demanded who employ'd him, or how he came there?

"Why, I was sent, sir, by the Company of Undertakers," says he, "and they were employed by the honest gentleman, who is executor to the good Doctor departed."

Dr. John Partridge
1708

The name of Isaac Bickerstaff Steele borrowed from his friend Swift*, who, just before the establishment of the "Tatler," had borrowed it from a shoemaker's shop-board, and used it as the name of an imagined astrologer, who should be an astrologer indeed, and should attack John Partridge, the chief of the astrological almanack makers, with a definite prediction of the day and hour of his death. This he did in a pamphlet that brought up to the war against one stronghold of superstition an effective battery of satire. The joke once set rolling was kept up in other playful little pamphlets written to announce the fulfilment of the prophecy, and to explain to Partridge that, whether he knew it or not, he was dead.

From Henry Morely's Introduction to *Isaac Bickerstaff: Physician and Astrologer*
Richard Steele
1709

∞ *AN EPITAPH ON PARTRIDGE* ∞

Here, five Foot deep, lies on his Back,
A Cobler, Starmonger, and Quack;
Who to the Stars in pure Good-will,
Does to his best look upward still.
Weep all you Customers that use
His Pills, his Almanacks, or Shoes;
And you that did your Fortunes seek,
Step to his Grave but once a Week:
This Earth which bears his Body's Print,
You'll find has so much Vertue in't,
That I durst pawn my Ears 'twill tell
Whate'er concerns you full as well,
In Physick, Stolen Goods, or Love,
As he himself could, when above.

Jonathan Swift

---

*   Ever the enemy of humbug and ignorance, Dean Swift created the character of Isaac Bickerstaff to ridicule astrology and, especially, the astrologer John Partridge, whose death Bickerstaff predicted with the inaccuracy common to his profession.
    The hoax extended beyond Swift, with Richard Steele appointing the fictitious Bickerstaff as editor of his new magazine the *Tatler* and others using the name for their own satirical purposes.

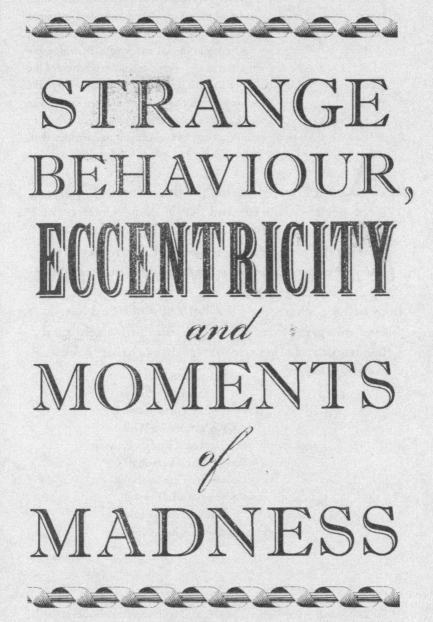

STRANGE
BEHAVIOUR,
ECCENTRICITY
and
MOMENTS
of
MADNESS

At any given moment, the population of Dublin is 20 per cent tourists and 80 per cent 'characters'. These 'characters' live in a heightened state of being, finding the world funnier, stranger, more beguiling than mere people do, and they are unable to keep this fact to themselves. While not every citizen may admit to being a 'character', they all know one and have at least one great story of that person's unconventional behaviour and eccentric passage through this crooked, twisting city.

Peter Marsh of Dublin, Esq.; died of a conceit that he was mad. Four months before, as he was riding out, a hoarse in the Staggers took hold of him by the Breeches, shook him, and laid him on the Ground, without the least Harm. Three Weeks after, being told that the Horse was dead of the Staggers, he said "The Horse dy'd mad, and I shall die mad too." In this Persuasion he persisted to his Death, tho' he had no other Symptoms of Madness, nor sign thereof in his Body when opened.

Gentleman's Magazine and Historical Chronicle
Vol. 10, 1740

SOMNAMBULISM

Edward Harding, a student of Trinity College, Dublin, who inhabited an attic in the left wing of the University, was in the habit of walking upon the roof in his sleep. One night, having taken a relation, who was locked out, to sleep with him, they had not been in bed more than two hours, when the latter saw him deliberately get up, put on his clothes, strike a light, and sit down, apparently to study. This, however, did not surprise him, as he thought his friend was preparing for the approaching examinations. In a few moments, he observed him opening the window and immediately proceeding to walk out of it upon the roof. Recollecting that his friend had the habit of sleep-walking, he pursued him cautiously. The day was just dawning and he could see him distinctly walking along the parapet with destruction within an inch of him. Actuated with strong fear for his friend's safety, he proceeded in the gutter of the roof, until he came behind Mr. Harding, who now stood at the extreme end of the building and seemed to look down upon the distant earth with the greatest sang froid and, seizing him suddenly by the arm, pulled upon him into the gutter, there holding him by force, notwithstanding his violent exertions to disengage himself until at length he became quite awake and sensible of his perilous situation. He never afterwards walked in his sleep, although he used to get out of bed at night and mope about for a moment or two but he would awake in the greatest terror, which, however, soon dissipated, and he rested well the remainder of the night.

Dublin Penny Journal
June 14th, 1834

DOCTOR BARRETT
Late Senior Fellow and Vice-Provost of Trinity College, Dublin

His eccentricities cannot be duly appreciated by those who have never seen him.

Notwithstanding his immense wealth, so strong was his passion for hoarding money that he never burned a candle in the evening, unless when engaged in writing or some other occupation which rendered one absolutely necessary and, even then, he put it out the moment he was done. Dr. Elrington, the present professor of divinity, when a student in college called on him one evening for a book. Barrett led the way up stairs in the dark, into a large room, where after groping about for some time he found a book of the same size as the one for which he was searching. "D'ye see me now," he said, as he gave it, "go back with this book and see if it is the right one and, if it is not, bring it back to me and I'll light a candle to look for it for you."

The same parsimonious feeling caused him considerable trouble whenever he examined, at fellowship or scholarship examination, which he did every year when a senior fellow. He wore a profusion of his own hair turned up before and curled upon a buckle behind, like a wig; this he used carefully to powder at every examination and at no other time and he appeared on the bench conspicuous for a very white head and a very dirty shirt. When the examination was over, he carefully combed out the powder into a sheet of paper and kept it till the next year.

Dublin University Magazine
Vol. 18, July to December 1841

A crowd of wrestlers had assembled near me, a regular ring had been formed and, on the verge of this ring, upon his small bay pony, appeared that pink of gymnastic amateurs, the eccentric Dr. Brennan. Of this gentleman I had already heard much: he is one of those whom the Dublin wags denominate 'dusts' or oddities of the town. He writes pleasantly, prescribes readily, charges moderately, and, by those who could relish low humour, might be looked upon as rather an agreeable boon companion. Some say that he possesses skill, but that the bluntness of his manners and the vulgarity of his habits have kept him from rising in his profession. In his practice, also, as a physician, there are some peculiarities: he is as much attached to the prescribing of turpentine as Sangrado was to hot water.

Dublin and London Magazine
June 1825

AN ARISTOCRATIC POLICEMAN.
A BARONET WHO WEARS THE UNIFORM.

It is not generally known that the holder of one of the baronetcies in Ireland is at present a policeman, serving in the Constabulary Depot, Dublin. This is Sir Thomas Echlin, Bart., the seventh baronet of the name, and the lineal descendant of Sir Henry Echlin, second Baron of the Exchequer, who was created a Baronet of the Kingdom of Ireland on the 17th of October, 1721. The family were at one time in possession of large estates in the counties of Dublin, Kildare, Carlow, and Galway; but, like many another Irish family, they were brought to ruin by extravagant living and costly lawsuits. The fifth and sixth baronets were poor illiterate agricultural labourers in the County of Kildare. The present baronet succeeded to the title on the death of his father, Sir Ferdinand-Fenton Echlin (who, like his father, was a labourer), in 1877, being then, as now, a member of the Royal Irish Constabulary. On his succession to the baronetage, he was transferred from the country station, where he was doing duty as a constable, to the depot, Phoenix Park. He is now a sergeant, and employed as a clerk in the commandant's office.

Belfast Evening Telegraph
August 19th, 1895

COLLEGE STREET POLICE OFFICE.
A MONOMANIAC IN DUBLIN.

On Monday, Sergeant Durham charged a young man, who gave his name as William Boadley, with loitering in the neighbourhood of Haddington-road, at the hour of two o'clock upon the morning of Monday, with the intent (as he supposed) to commit a felony. It appeared that the sergeant found the prisoner in a hall and, when spoken to, he could not give a satisfactory account of himself. The prisoner, who appeared to be labouring under a mental disorder, when called upon for his defence by Mr. Tyndall, said he was a shoemaker, a native of Donegal, who came to Dublin on his way to London to see the Queen; because he was credibly informed by some gentlemen, that if she once saw him she would be so struck with his appearance as to give him some appointment in her household, but his money falling short he was not able to proceed. Mr. Tyndal committed him for fifteen days in default of finding bail.

Banner of Ulster
April 14th, 1843

SHOCKING SELF-MUTILATION.

A horrible attempt, it is supposed, to commit suicide was made in a field near the Grand Canal, Dublin, on Sept. 3, by a gentleman whose family occupy a good position in the Irish capital. Mr. James E. Gannon, a medical student, aged 36, residing in the suburbs of Kingstown, had been suffering from delusions and left home in the morning, his brother, with whom he lodged, however, not noticing anything in his demeanour to create alarm. Mr. Gannon seems to have made his way to Dublin, and about one o'clock a little girl saw him walking across a field. He was holding a pocket handkerchief to his eyes, which were bleeding. The girl called the attention of her mother, who found Gannon lying down. She assisted him up, and guided the unhappy man to her house, where she perceived that he was sightless, his eyes having disappeared altogether. The medical men found that both eyes had been taken out of their sockets, and there was ample evidence that the injuries had been self-inflicted.

Mr. Gannon would have taken his degree as doctor next month. Over-study, it is supposed, unbalanced his mind.

Maitland Mercury, Maitland NSW
October 18th, 1888

In 1810, the Bow Street Distillery became the property of a father and son, both called John Jameson. John Jameson and Son Irish Whiskey Company became, under that ownership, the world's most popular whiskey, producing a million gallons a year and making the two Johns very wealthy men. When the titular son had a son of his own, the young James S. Jameson, he raised him with every privilege, opportunity, and legal excuse that money could buy.

THE HORRIBLE JAMESON AFFAIR
*ASSAD FARRAN TELLS HIS STORY OF THE CANNIBALISM**

The *Times* publishes the full text of Assad Farran's affidavit. After describing Barttelot's cruelties, it deals with the Jameson cannibal affair at Ribakiba.

Jameson expressed to Tippoo's interpreter curiosity to witness cannibalism. Tippoo consulted with the chiefs and told Jameson he had better purchase a slave. Jameson asked the price and paid six handkerchiefs.

A man returned a few minutes afterward with a ten-year-old girl. Tippoo and the chiefs ordered the girl to be taken to the native huts. Jameson himself, Selim, Masondie, and Farhani, Jameson's servant, presented to him by Tippoo, and many others followed.

The man who had brought the girl said to the cannibals: "This is a present from a white man who desires to see her eaten."

"The girl was tied to a tree," says Farran, "the natives sharpening their knives the while. One of them then stabbed her twice in the belly.

"She did not scream, but knew what would happen, looking to the right and left for help. When stabbed she fell dead. The natives cut pieces from her body.

"Jameson, in the meantime, made rough sketches of the horrible scenes. Then we all returned to the chief's house. Jameson afterward went to his tent, where he finished his sketches in water colors.

"There were six of them, all neatly done. The first sketch was of the girl as she was led to the tree. The second showed her stabbed, with the blood gushing from the wounds. The third showed her dissected. The fourth, fifth, and sixth showed men carrying off the various parts of the body.

"Jameson showed these and many other sketches to all the chiefs."

New York Times
November 14th, 1890

---

* A response from Jameson's widow, defending her husband, appeared in the *New York Times* the next day. It consisted of a letter composed by Jameson, on his death bed, at Stanley Falls in 1888. The letter, written two years before the *New York Times* article appeared, challenges the central hideous accusation while corroborating some minor details.

Samara Leibner

THE LIE

There was, in the Cathedral of Christchurch, Dublin, a Marble Image of Christ, with a Reed in his Hand, and a Crown of Thorns on his Head. While the English Service was said before the Lord Lieutenant, the Archbishop of Dublin, the Privy Council, the Mayor of the City, and a great Assembly, Blood was seen to run down the Crevices of the Crown of Thorns and to trickle down the Face of the Image, whereupon some of the Contrivers of the Fraud cried out, See how our Saviour's Image Sweats Blood, which it could not but do, since Heresy is now come into the Church; whereat several of the common People fell down with Beads in their Hands, and prayed to the Image; vast Numbers flockt to the Sight and the confusion was so great that the Congregation broke up and the Lord Lieutenant and Council hastened out of the Quire, for fear of Danger.

The Archbishop of Dublin, suspecting the Cheat, caused the Image to be searched and washed, to see if it would bleed afresh: Which was no sooner done, but a Spunge was found within the Hollow of the Image's Head – Which Leigh (some time a Monk of that Cathedral) had soak'd in a Bowl of Blood and, watching his Opportunity, early on Sunday Morning, had placed the Spunge so swoln with Blood over the Image's Head, within the Crown, and so, by little and little, the Blood soaked through upon the Face.

The Spunge was presently brought down and shewed to those Worshippers, who were both ashamed, and cursed Father Leigh and the Contrivers of the Cheat, who were all put to publick Penance the next Sunday in the Church and stood on a Table before the Pulpit, with their Crime written on their Breasts – the Archbishop of Dublin himself, Preaching before the Lord Lieutenant and Council, chose for his Text that remarkable and seasonable Portion of Holy Scripture, taken out of the 2 Thess ii. II.: "God shall send them strong Delusions that they should believe a Lye."

God's Goodness Visible in our Deliverance from Popery
Henry Maule
1733

EXTRAORDINARY RELATION
OF GREAT ABSTINENCE AND SUPERNATURAL EXPERIENCE

Dublin, July 25th, 1809.

Mrs. W----, a widow, about thirty years ago was confined to bed by a general debility of her frame and loss of appetite, during which she retained such health and spirits, as made her fasting appear very extraordinary. Those about her heard her with astonishment talk of seeing angels and perceived that her abstaining from gross food was, for the most part, voluntary, for several weeks together. She was now removed to the house of one who observed these particulars, partly through curiosity, and partly through charity, as she was very poor. Every means were used to detect imposition and she lived on bread-tea for two months. A strict watch was kept over her and she took no other food; the consequence was that her emaciation increased to an extreme; her skin was uncommonly white and she was rather handsome with dark expressive eyes and delicate features. She was often perceived to wave about her right arm, as if taking something from an invisible hand; and, indeed, the extreme whiteness and emaciation of her arm made her not seem of mortal mould.

She had visions of Heaven and appeared so spiritualized that the specific gravity of her body was balanced by the internal buoyancy and before several witnesses she rose up in a horizontal position; and frequently sat up without the aid of her arms in rising, which would have been impossible to mere nature in her weak state.

One morning, she sent for the lady of the house. She appeared to have passed the night in great horror of mind; her looks were wild and despairing, instead of the sweet placid beauty of her countenance, which had hitherto been remarkable for serenity. She said "I am a deceiver! all I have said was imagination and lies!" She was then interrogated in all she formerly professed and she accounted for it as delusion; or acquired from books. She left that house and in a month was seen begging; in some time after she got into a prosperous livelihood, was married to a soldier, had a child, and appeared to be of a devout and reputable character to her death.

Supernatural Magazine
September 1809

THE MAN WHO COUNTS

Miler wears a long grey overcoat down to his heels, demonstrating that he was dressed by a very careless tailor. Miler was an original and showed it on one day in the week, Sunday; on that day, he was always to be found in Church Street, engaged in the peculiar occupation of counting the bars in the railings which circle around the Four Courts from Church Street to Chancery Place – no mean task, as the number of rails must total several hundreds, if not thousands, yet Miler would put his forefinger upon each in turn. Many said that he was mad, others inclined to the belief that he was a wise fool; who knows which opinion was right.

Dublin Historical Record
December 1939

The homes and streets of Dublin have been filled, always, with the pious, the penitent, and the religiously devout. In their devotion, they are spurred on to behaviour that the earthly among us might find inconvenient at best.

In early Christian Ireland, every learned person was a saint, but there were many fewer saints as the centuries rolled on. The city's own Matt Talbot has not been officially recognised as such, although declared Venerable by the church. A miracle performed in his name is currently under investigation and he remains a patron and inspiration to those fighting addiction. However, the extent of his ascetic rebuttal of the demon drink was not fully known until after his death.

DEATH AND PREPARATION

Matt Talbot was passing along the footpath, when Mrs. Keogh, coming out of the doorway adjoining her store, saw him fall. She called her son and both ran over to where he lay, lifted him and carried him to the hall door beside the store from which she had come, intending to bring him into the store. Seeing that he was very pale and unable to speak she entered the shop to get some water which she brought out. Then lifting his head to give him a drink, she realised that it was not a faintness but that he was dying. As she put the cup of water to his lips she said, "My poor fellow, you are going to Heaven." Matt Talbot opened his eyes and stared at her very earnestly, but did not speak. He then laid his head down, and as she withdrew her hand from under it, he died.

A man who was returning from the church came over to where Matt Talbot lay and blessed him with the crucifix. Father Walsh, O.P., came from the church, and seeing that he was dead, knelt in the lane and recited prayers. Later on the Corporation ambulance arrived and the body was removed to the mortuary attached to Jervis Street Hospital (Sisters of Mercy), which was close by. Here later on in the morning, Sister Ignatius, Sister of Mercy, came with a nurse and the hospital porters to prepare the body for burial. As Sister Ignatius was cutting away the clothes the scissors struck something hard, which, on further investigation, proved to be the chains which bound the body around the waist. With reverence, not unmixed with awe, they removed the chains and ropes and the big beads with its crucifix which always rested against his heart. The chains were rusty but the body was scrupulously clean. Then dressing the body in the brown habit of St. Francis, they placed it in the coffin with the chains, ropes and medals.

Life of Matt Talbot
Sir Joseph Glynn
1928

PIOUS ZOZIMUS THE POET

"Zozimus" a man not less familiarly known in Dublin than Solomon Eagle was in London. His real name, as appears from the cemetery records, was Michael Moran. This man boasted that he walked in the footsteps of Homer and was as well known in Dublin as Nelson's Pillar. What old citizen does not remember that tall, gaunt, blind man, dressed in a heavy, long-tailed coat and a dinged high hat, armed with a blackthorn stick, secured to his wrist by a thong and finished by an iron ferule?

Evening after evening, Zozimus made his pilgrimage through the streets, advancing with slow and measured steps and halting at intervals to collect in his hat the alms of the faithful. His great popular recitation was "The Life, Conversion, and Death of St. Mary of Egypt, who was discovered in the Wilderness in the Fifth Century by pious Zozimus."

A sham "Zoz" once took his rounds on the same night as the real man and created quite a sensation on Essex (now Grattan) Bridge, where both met and their sonorous tones mingled, to the confusion of their respective followers. On this occasion the real man called the other an "impostherer," but the latter gave back the epithet and touchingly complained of the heartlessness of mocking a poor dark man. Words ran high and the sham "Zoz" said, "Good Christians, just give me a grip of that villian and I'll soon let him know who the real impostherer is." Then pretending to give his victim a "guzzler," he pressed some silver into his hand and vanished.

Mozart, on his death-bed, composed his own requiem, which skilled musicians took down from dictation. The Rev. Nicholas O Farrell, who was summoned to attend Zozimus when dying, stated that he found the room crowded with ballad-singers and Zozimus "dictatin'." Amongst other directions for his funeral said to have fallen from him were:

> I have no coronet to go before me,
> Nor Bucephalius that ever bore me ;
> But put my hat and stick and gloves together,

That bore for years the very worst of weather,
And rest assured in spirit will be there
Mary of Agypt and Susannah fair.
And Pharoah's daughter with the heavenly blushes
That took the drowning goslin from the rushes.
I'll not permit a tomb-stone stuck above me,
Nor effigy; but, boys, if still yees love me,
Build a nate house for all whose fate is hard,
And give a bed to every wanderin' bard.

Michael Moran had reached the age of only 43, and he died from pulmonary disease, the result of exposure to severe weather. Two portraits of this strange character are extant, one by Henry MacManus, R.H.A.,the other by Mr. Horatio Nelson. He was buried on Palm Sunday, the 5th April, 1846.

History of the Cemeteries of Dublin
William Fitzpatrick
1900

CAPTAIN DEMPSEY,
THE HERMIT OF DUBLIN

Who that was resident in Dublin between the last forty and fifty years but remembers Captain Dempsey? — a tall, sinewy man, with high cheek bones, sunken eyes, and self-resigned aspect, and over whose chin no razor had passed for years. His beard was of a brownish hue and very bushy. He wore in general a long plaid mantle tied at the neck, and hanging loosely over his shoulders — a broad hat, with a singularly round crown; two patches of leather sewed on his knees, and large silver buckles in his shoes. His finger was adorned with several rings — not for their lustre, it was evident, but in remembrance of some dear friends; for at times he would be seen to make a sudden stand in the streets, look on them with a wild stare, then, as if collecting his scattered senses together, let the day be never so wet, drop to his knees, offer up on each ring a prayer in silence, then precipitately rise and proceed on his journey, although through a crowd of gapers and shouts of idle boys. Patrick-street was his favourite haunt, and he seemed to have a particular taste for herrings, as he was seldom ever observed to return home without a few of them under his cloak.

His habitation was a wooden hut, in one corner of a piece of waste ground, at the lower end of Townsend-street, near the old depot. The door

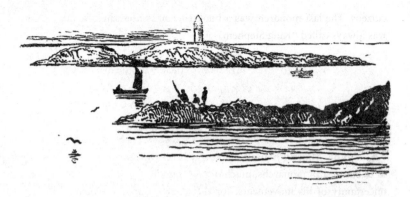

was at the top, to which he ascended by blocks of wood nailed at the outside at regular distances. The door or window, we may call it either, overlooked the sea: there would he sit for hours together in seeming pensiveness. When his mind would be tranquil, which was often the case, he was very conversant, and so condescending to the enquiry of the curious, that he would seem gratified in satisfying the inquisitive demands of the meanest boy. But if any of his fits of insanity should visit him, he would clap the door in the face of the person to whom he was speaking, and retire to a place he had under ground, in which was a little altar, and two tin lamps constantly burning. Sometimes his door would be shut for several days, until the fit worked off him, for which the neighbours charitably watched, and as soon as he again appeared and resumed his accustomed station, would bring him such refreshments as his weak frame required. The chief point requisite in the visitor appeared to be to keep his mind and eyes from his rings; for if he once dwelt on them all discourse was over, and ten chances to one but the door of his little habitation would be so quickly dashed in the face of the visitor, as to strike him violently in the face.

Dublin Penny Journal
February 21st, 1835

THE KING OF DALKEY AND OTHER OFFICERS OF STATE

A convivial society some years ago existed in Dublin, who periodically assembled at the island of Dalkey and elected a king and other officers of state. A column of this paper was always devoted to their proceedings, which were then interesting, as the society comprised a number of respectable citizens. The last monarch was a bookseller of the name of Armitage, who was always called "King Stephen."

History of the City of Dublin
John Warburton and James Whitelaw
1818

HIS MAJESTY

As to his Majesty himself, he was at times the gravest, and at times the merriest of monarchs, much of his humour consisting in the whimsical uncertainty of his movements, for there never was a crowned head more capricious or changeable in disposition than the King of Dalkey. He would set out attended by his court on a journey to some distant region of his dominion, change his mind in a minute and alter his route elsewhere and again change in a few minutes; and all these mutations of purpose were most loyally approved of and sympathised in by his majesty's nobles and subjects. Another trait in King Stephen's character was his love for song; and when the word ran through his empire that at the royal banquet his majesty had commenced or was about to commence his favourite "Love is my passion and glory!" there was scarcely one of his subjects, male or female, who did not make a rush to get within ear-shot of him. Peace be with thee, Stephen! thou wert a king of "infinite jest and most excellent fancy;" and although thy reign was short and thy dominions small, thou mad'st more of thy subjects truly happy than many monarchs whose reigns were as much longer as their possessions were more extensive!

The king landed in state and was saluted by ordnance on the island. He assembled the most convivial members of the society under the names of his principal officers, and the other guests as his subjects, and in a mock heroic speech resigned his crown into their hands, and desired them to elect a successor.

The last meeting of the convivial society of which the King of Dalkey was president, and which formerly attracted so large a portion of public attention, was held on the 20th August 1797.

Illustrated Dublin Journal
March 29th, 1862

— OLD DUBLIN SOCIETY TO VISIT DALKEY —

The Old Dublin Society on Saturday next will visit the Kingdom of Dalkey or the Port of the Seven Castles. The visit will coincide with

the anniversary of the coronation of the president of the society, Alderman T. Kelly T.D. in 1934 as "King of Dalkey, Emperor of the Muglins, Prince of the Holy Island of Magee, and Elector of Lambay and Ireland's Eye, Defender of his own Faith and Respector of all others and Sovereign of the Most Illustrious Order of the Lobster and Periwinkle".

July 18th, 1940

"Lord of all Dalkey lands,
Chief of our jovial bands,
Are you not man?
With you though peace doth reign,
Nor blood your isle doth stain,
Nor famine here complain,
Are you not man?

What though the realms rejoice
In your melodious voice;
Kings are but men!
And while each subject sings:
'God made us men, not kings!'
With echo Dalkey rings:
'Kings are but men!'"

A traditional Dalkenian air
1793

MAN, WOMAN AND CHILD

The traditional Irish family was a complex machine that always threatened to break. No wonder so many parents were well-oiled.

The lives of women and children were undervalued, even while their stations were exalted, and the lives of working men were stressful and brutal. The youngest person imprisoned in Kilmainham was five years old* and many other children lost their parents to exile, with men and women shipped off to Australia. Parents lost their children to sickness, accident, and cruelty. And some were just lost.

---

* This was Catherine Lyons who was imprisoned for a week, with her family, for travelling without a train ticket, in 1855.

GIRLS' PROTECTION CRUSADE
AGAINST THE WHITE SLAVE TRAFFIC

Presidents:
THE COUNTESS OF FINGALL.
THE LADY HOMEPATRICK.

Vice-Presidents
MRS. GLASFORD ST. LAWRENCE.
MISS BARRETT.

Hon. Treasurers
JAMES TALBOT POWER, Esq., D.J.,

Asst. Hon. Treasurer
THE DOWAGER LADY GRACE

Hon. Solicitor
NORRIS GODDARD, Esq., J.P.

Hon. Medical Adviser
DR. ELLA WEBB

Published in 1913

TO THE EDITOR OF THE IRISH TIMES

Sir, A year ago we were organising our society and we think we should tell the public (who responded generously to our first appeal) something of our progress. Since issuing that appeal five workers have been specially trained and have been constantly employed in meeting girls at the various Dublin railway stations and also at the boats.

They have, in nine months, helped by their advice and protection 1801 girls in Dublin alone. For the most part, these were Irish country girls, inexperienced in the ways of cities, with no friends in Dublin who could help them and, in many instances, were almost or quite penniless. A few were French, German, Austrian, Norwegian, and Japanese. It can readily be seen how easily such girls would fall into bad hands. Of this we have proof and our work is to make every effort to prevent such deplorable misfortune. Our warning notices are posted up in fifty-seven railway stations. In addition to their warning paragraphs, they give addresses in Dublin where girls can find safe lodgings, etc.

We gratefully acknowledge in your advertising columns subscriptions received since our last public acknowledgement and desire specially to thank the Girls' Friendly Society,

the Mothers' Union, and the Society of Friends for their
generous contributions of the salaries of two workers. As
our outlay is of necessity considerable, we urgently request
continued monetary support.

 Yours, etc.

TO THE EDITOR OF THE IRISH TIMES

Sir, May we ask your help to warn parents against sending
their girls to London to persons advertising offers to
teach dressmaking, etc.? Some terrible experiences have
lately been laid before us. We would recommend parents
first to apply to the clergy of their own parish, who,
through clerical colleagues in London, will generally be
able to report as to the good faith of advertisers. Failing
information from that source, the Church Army will give all
possible help.

 Yours, etc.

Irish Times
December 10th, 1913

⤜ *MAKING BABIES BY STEAM* ⤜

You lovers of mirth, I pray pay attention
And listen to what I am going to relate,
Concerning a couple I overheard talking
As I was returning late home from a wake.
As I looked around I espied an old woman
Who sat by a gap all a-minding her cow.
She was jigging a tune called "Come haste to the wedding"
Or some other ditty I can't recall now,
She was jigging a tune called "An Buachaillín Donn"
Or some other ditty I can't tell you now.

Then, in looking around, I espied a bold tinker
Who only by chance came a-passing that way.
The weather being warm, he sat down to rest,
"Oh what news, honest man?" the old woman did say.
"Oh, it's no news at all, ma'am," replied the bold tinker,
"But there's one and I wish he never had been.
It's that damnable rogue of a Daniel O'Connell,
He's now making children in Dublin by steam."

"Our children are ruined," replied the old woman.
"Ainm an diabhal! is he crazy at last?
Is there sign of a war or a sudden rebellion
Or what is the reason he wants them so fast?"
"Oh, it's not that at all, ma'am," replied the bold tinker,
"But the children of Ireland are getting so small,
It's her majesty's petition to the Lord High Lieutenant
To not let us make them the old way at all."

"By each hair on my head," replied the old woman,
"And that's the great oath of my soul, for to say!
I am an old woman, but, if I were nigh him,
It's little a word that O'Connell might say.
The people of Ireland, it's very well-known,
We gave him our fortunes, though needing them bad
And now he is well-compensating us for it;
He's taking what little diversion we had!"

"I am an old woman that's going on eighty,
Scarcely a hair on my head to be seen,
But, if the villain provokes me, I'll make better children
Than ever he could produce with his steam!"
"Good luck to you, woman," replied the bold tinker,
"Long may you live and have youth on your side.
For, if all the young women of Ireland were like you,
O'Connell might soon shove his engine one side"

"I think every woman who is in this country
Should be out making babies as fast as she can.
So, if ever Her Majesty calls for an army,
We'll be able to send her as many as Dan."

Trad.

REVOLTING BARBARITY

Patrick McSweeney complained against Patrick Owens, under the following circumstances: The parties lodged in the same house No. 28, Denmark-street. The complainant stated that, on Sunday evening last, some children of his family were in the kitchen which was beneath the parlour occupied by the defendant. The latter, with a heated poker, made a hole in one of the boards of the floor of his apartment and, through it, poured down

Samara Leibner

a quantity of boiling water, whereby some of them were scalded. He did not see this actually done, but he had reason to believe it to be a fact. One of the children who had been injured was then in the board room.

Mrs. Bridget Sweeney, the mother of the complainant, stated that the defendant admitted the fact in her presence and in that of a policeman, immediately after its occurrence.

The defendant complained that the children made such a noise as to disturb his wife, who, at the time, was lying seriously ill in the parlour. He had taken out a cross-summons against the complainant and his brother for threatening to assault him on the occasion. By a reply to a question from the bench, it appeared that the summons on the defendant's part had not been taken out till after service on him of that of the plaintiff.

After dismissing the cross-summons, the magistrates bound the defendant to keep the peace. Mr. Duffey expressed his regret that the charge against him had not been brought for an assault, as the bench in such case would have felt it its duty to inflict a very serious penalty on him, for conduct at once most cruel, inhuman, and utterly unjustifiable.

Freeman's Journal
February 29th, 1832

ATTEMPTED WIFE MURDER
STRANGE CASE IN DUBLIN

A shocking case was reported to the police at Santry, County Dublin, last night, in consequence of which Mr. Frank Molloy, proprietor of "The Arch," Henry Street, one of the biggest public-houses in Dublin, has been placed under arrest. Mr. Molloy was in his place of business on Christmas Day and, in the evening, drove to his residence, The Hall, Santry. An hour later, an ambulance was summoned and Mrs Molloy was removed to the Mater Miseracordiae Hospital, where it was found that her throat had been badly cut with a razor. She lies in a serious condition and very little hope is entertained of her recovery. In the forenoon, it was thought advisable to take a statement from her before a Magistrate who attended specially at the hospital. It is said that, when the police visited his residence during the night, they found Mr. Molloy in an excited state. The parties are in good circumstances. Mr. Molloy, it is said, without any previous altercation, followed his wife to her bedroom and, it is alleged, cut her throat. Afterwards, he called one of his sons, who immediately took his mother to a car to have her removed to hospital. Mr. Molloy meanwhile sent the gatekeeper to tell the police.

Glasgow Herald
December 27th, 1912

INTERFERING BETWEEN MAN AND WIFE

Constable 218 D charged Mary Mathews and Margaret, her daughter, with assaulting him and obstructing him in the discharge of his duty.

The plaintiff stated that on Thursday, while on duty in Church-street, he observed a great crowd of persons about the door of Mr. Mathews' shop in the same street. He immediately went to the place and there he saw Mrs. M. inside, stripped, fighting with her husband, and breaking the windows. Having dispersed the crowd in the first instance, he entered the place to give Mrs. M. some quiet advice, but, the moment he opened his mouth, she spat in his face and, letting go of the husband, hit him severely right and left about the neck and stomach. She then snatched up a knife and swore she would run it through his body. He ran out of the place immediately, in order to bring assistance to have her taken into custody, but, on his return and attempting to pass in, the daughter shut the half door of the shop against him and, with her clenched fists, struck him several blows across it. In consequence of the resistance he encountered, he was finally compelled to go away without having executed his duty.

Mr. Duffy – Did the husband take any part in the affray as between you and the other parties?

Plaintiff – No, indeed, Your Worship, I must say that the poor man behaved himself peaceably enough in that respect. When the wife let go her grip of him and, while they were cuffing me, he only stood out of the way and cried out, "Oh, Mary, Mary, you terrible Tory you. Is it smashing a policeman you are and he executing his duty?"

Freeman's Journal
March 8th, 1841

MISCELLANEOUS MATRIMONY, Draper, age 23, R.C. with £100 cash, good appearance and address, is anxious to meet young Lady with business or Land of her own; view early marriage; *young widow not objected*; strictest secrecy.

MATRIMONY, GENTLEMAN, 25, 5ft 6ins, possessing private income over £140 a year, inheriting several thousand pounds later, desires correspondence, view Matrimony, with young Lady with private income; she must be very tall and well-educated; also a Catholic; as this is absolutely genuine, no Lady need fear to answer; *her letters will be treated with secrecy.*

Freeman's Journal
December 7th, 1909

A STRANGE STORY IN HIGH LIFE

A widow residing in Rathmines had two sons and three daughters, the latter highly accomplished and beautiful. The family was held in the highest respect and visited much among the aristocracy of the city. The eldest daughter was a finished musician, clever artist, and an admirable tennis player. She attended all the fashionable festivities, where she was always conspicuous. Two months ago the mother announced that this young lady was going to London to study drawing. She returned, on Christmas, in the apparel of a young man. The mother then informed the astonished friends that the child was a boy. The incident has caused a great perturbation in families where the quondam girl visited and the public curiosity is highly excited in the district where the family live. The child had been treated as a girl from infancy and dressed and behaved as a lady. No explanation is given.

Quebec Daily Telegraph
January 4th, 1888

CHILD MURDER

We rejoice that the subject of child-murder has been brought thus palpably before the public. As a social evil it yields to none and, indeed, might be called par excellence the great social evil of the day ... for although the public mind has been disturbed by the increasing prevalence of infanticide and by the daily horrors with which it is but too familiar, yet there is such an appearance of indecision regarding the proper steps to be adopted ... Every paper we take up, every publication which purports to chronicle the passing events of the day, shows that the evil has spread to an alarming extent.

Dublin Review
1858

MURDER OF A CHILD BY ITS MOTHER

On the 7th and 8th instant, the coroner of the county Dublin held an inquest at Lucan, on the body of a child, one month old, named Elizabeth Nolan. It appeared in evidence that two of the Leixlip constabulary were passing between Banbuster Bridge and Lucan, when one of them observed a child in the canal. He called to his comrade, when he took the child out who was then warm. The other policeman observed a woman running swiftly, whom he overtook in a quarter of an hour. She immediately acknowledged that she was the mother, and said that she committed the unfortunate act from want. The prisoner has been committed to Kilmainham.

Banner of Ulster
June 17th, 1842

CHILD-STRIPPING VAGRANTS

An elderly woman of forbidding appearance was brought up in the custody of Sergeant Daly of the G division of police, charged with having inveigled a female child of about three years of age into a hall in

Townsend-street and having there stripped the poor infant of her clothes with which she (the prisoner) ran off, leaving the child in a state of perfect nudity.

Freeman's Journal
December 14th, 1852

FIENDISH ATTEMPT AT CHILD MURDER

A DEED of terrible and, we are glad to say, of rare atrocity, was attempted on Friday last, at a place known as the "Back of the Pipes". A poor little child, having wandered away from its mother's door, was seized by a strange woman, who, without any exaggeration, we may term a fiend in female form. The wretch stripped the child of its clothes and threw it into the water through a trap. Luckily, the water was low and the stream flowed more sluggishly than usual, otherwise nothing could have saved the child from being swept away. Its screams, as it lay in the water, protected from being carried onward by some obstruction, were heard by some persons who were passing. On Saturday, the clothes of which the child had been bereft were found in a pawn office where they had been pawned for two or three shillings. In presence of such diabolical iniquity, one stands horror-stricken and silent. It is hard to imagine any human being so hardened and depraved, hard to conceive how any woman with a human heart in her bosom could have been deaf to the piteous cries of the infant whom she deliberately flung to death with the ferocity and cruelty of a very demon.

Irish Times
March 8th, 1879

EXHUMATION

In the Morning the Body of the white Negro Boy (lately exhibited as a Curiosity in this City) was dug up at the burying Ground near Island-bridge, where he had been interred the Night before. From some Marks of Violence that appeared on him 'tis imagined he was murdered.

Freeman's Journal
May 14th, 1765

THE BABY

The new-born infant discovered in Christ Church yard on Tuesday night had no marks of violence on the body, but was very black in the face;

the woman detected in slooping near where the child was laid is well known to be of an infamous character; and the entire of the transaction will very possibly be found out.

Freeman's Journal
March 3rd, 1804

CHILD DESERTION

Roger McGuiness, John Hannigan, and Patrick Macken, overseers of deserted children for Thomas's parish, appeared on summons to answer the complaint of Sarah Williams, for refusing to compensate her for the maintenance and burial of a child found deserted in their parish about ten days back and which died on Friday evening.

The child, it appeared, had, in the first instance, been ordered by the magistrates to be left with the overseers of St. Mary's parish, it being represented as having been found within the district and Mr. Christopher Coyne, one of the overseers, afforded some temporary aid towards its subsistence. He, however, subsequently discovered and now showed that the unfortunate infant had been actually abandoned within the bounds of the parish of St. Thomas, though immediately on the verge of that of St. Mary.

Proof was given of due notice to the defendants of their liability to the support of the infant. The claim against them was five shillings for ten day's maintenance and six shillings for the interment of the infant.

Freeman's Journal
March 8th, 1841

ATTEMPTED KIDNAP

On the 14th of March last, four little children, the eldest aged nine years, the youngest but four, were placed in a third-class carriage of the Midland Railway. They were fatherless and their mother, a Protestant, had found a friend who offered four of her orphans an asylum in the Protestant Orphanage of Galway. On the arrival of the train, two persons – Denis O'Connor and McRobins – appeared to have taken possession of the four children. Mrs. Harnett attempted to get possession of them, but was repelled by force. They were taken by these two men to a common lodging house at Galway, kept by one John O'Connor; and, though the mother herself, accompanied by the Rev. Mr. Brownrigg, demanded possession of them on that

Samara Leibner

evening, the O'Connors refused to deliver them up and denied her liberty to them.

The kidnappers made a rambling statement, to the effect that they were travelling, by accident, in the same train with the children, heard that their father was a Roman Catholic and that they determined to take charge of them.

The children were stolen on the 14th of March; on the 19th they were detained in defiance of the Queen's writ; and on the 22nd they are brought to Dublin by Thomas James McRobins, the Chairman of the Roman Catholic Dormitory, Townsend-street.

Irish Times
April 24th, 1860

TRACES OF STOLEN CHILDREN

No appearance was entered yesterday on the part of those who stole the four children of Mrs. Sherwood. The children are not forthcoming nor is there the smallest indication of the quarter to which they have been conveyed. In such a case as this, the detective police should be employed. It would be strange indeed to maintain at a very heavy cost a detective department, if its officers are either unwilling or unable to follow up the traces of four stolen children.

Irish Times
April 25th, 1860

LITTLE CHILDREN

Alicia and Patrick Murphy, the elder of whom is aged eleven, were in an orphan asylum near Dublin and they have disappeared; their mother liable to fund their retreat. The persons who last had custody of these children are supposed to be, and probably are, very respectable; they profess to  have no cognisance of the children's custody; and their personal character operates as a shield; while a certain indulgence is shown even for the extravagance of their conduct, since there is no doubt that in all these cases the motive is religious zeal.

The *Spectator*
May 5th, 1860

FASHIONABLE ATROCITY

This spiritual kidnapping seems to be the crime of the day in Ireland, the fashionable atrocity of the season. The Sherwood case is only one of three of the same description which are at this moment engaging the attention of the superior courts. There is also, as will be seen in our Irish news, a Murphy case and an Aylward case. The enthusiasm of the Irish for the Government of the Pope is a practical one; they copy what they devoutly admire, so that for one little Mortara at Bologna* we have no fewer than half a dozen in Dublin.

Launceston Examiner, Tasmania
July 14th, 1860

Margaret Aylward (1810–1889) was the founder of the Irish Sisters of the Holy Faith and of a Dublin branch of the Ladies of Charity of St. Vincent De Paul. In response to the death and mistreatment of foundlings and fostered babies across Dublin, she founded St. Brigid's Orphanage, Eccles Street, in 1857.

---

* Edgardo Levi Mortara was born and raised by an Italian Jewish family in Bologna. He was abducted by Papal authorities and adopted by Pope Pius IX, before becoming an Augustine priest in adulthood.

AT THE ORPHANAGE

The orphanage met with considerable difficulties and its enemies determined to destroy it. The means taken to do so were with regard to the admission of a child named Mary Mathews, whom her father had committed to the care of Miss Aylward, to be reared in the Catholic religion.

Miss Aylward was merely carrying out the intentions and will of the dying parent when she took upon herself the charge of the child. Mrs. Mathews, who became a Catholic at her marriage, came to the orphanage to demand her child. In the meantime, Mary Mathews had been taken from the nurse with whom Miss Aylward had placed her, without her knowledge, and, when asked for the child, she was able to declare that she never gave permission to anyone to take away the child and that it was quite impossible for her to restore it. The case was brought before the Judges and, after an investigation at the Crown Office, lasting only five days, Miss Aylward was brought before Judge Lefroy on 5th November 1860.

St. Brigid's Orphanage Annual Report
1897

THE OUTCOME OF THE CASE

We ventured to express an opinion, on Tuesday last, that had judgement been delivered in the case of Mathews against Aylward, we should not have had to comment on the case of the Sherwoods. Miss Aylward is the superioress of a Roman Catholic Orphanage in Eccles-street. Shortly after the matters connected with the abduction and concealment of Mary Mathews came before the Court of Queen's Bench, there was a large meeting convened in Malborough-street Chapel and a semi-religious service performed in honour of this orphanage. The Romish Archbishop extolled St. Bridgid's Society above all other societies and warmly commended the conduct of Miss Aylward.

Since that high festival, then, months have elapsed. The stolen child has not been restored nor can clue be found to the place of her imprisonment, justice has remained so long in abeyance. A heartless spinstress, who never felt the yearnings of maternal love and whose feelings were as stone to a mother's prayer for the restoration of her child, walked free and at large, triumphant over the law.

Irish Times
April 27th, 1860

Margaret Aylward was sentenced to six months imprisonment for contempt of court. She spent the first two days of her sentence in Richmond Bridewell, an all-male prison, where she was given her own room. It was decided that these conditions were too favourable and she was transferred to Grangegorman Female Penitentiary, where she was denied exercise and fresh air for four months.

"THE KIDNAPPING CASES"

The whole Tory Press is rampant about what are designed "the Kidnapping Cases." Wait a little, gentlemen, and you may find it necessary to pipe to a different tune. The first of those cases was finally adjudicated upon in the Court of Queen's Bench this day. It will be seen, by our report, that Mr. Corr made a return to the writ of habeas corpus, setting forth a will made by the father of the children, which, after making a pecuniary disposition about his family, confided the children to the guardianship of Mr. Corr, specifically directing that they should be left to the guardianship of Mr. Corr, in order that they should be educated in the Catholic religion. Mr. Corr, who has been denounced as one of the "kidnappers," was complimented in the most unqualified terms by Lord Chief Justice Lefroy, for his conduct in the whole affair and the satisfactory return he made to the court.

The Court directed that the children are to remain in the care of their guardian, Mr. Corr.

Dublin Evening Post
May 5th, 1860

MYSTERIOUS DISAPPEARANCE OF A CHILD

The young girl, Mary Carroll, who was stolen from her parents at No. 8 Castle-street, on Friday last, has not since been found. The woman with whom she was last seen has not yet been discovered by the police who are making active search in every part of the city. The mother of the child has offered a reward which will be paid to any person who will give such information as will lead to the discovery of the girl.

Irish Times
August 26th, 1864

ELLEN CARROLL

A subscription has been commenced to raise a sum sufficiently large to tempt one of the many who must, directly or indirectly, have some knowledge of the parties who stole this child to come forward and give information. The child, a little girl only 4 years old, was stolen on the 19th August and, although information was promptly given to the police and to every person whom the bereaved parents thought likely to aid them in their search, no trace of the child has as yet been found.

Irish Times
October 6th, 1864

MYSTERIOUS DISAPPEARANCE IN DUBLIN

A respectable young girl, aged fifteen, the daughter of a sergeant in the Dublin police, has, within the last few days, mysteriously disappeared. She left for home one evening last week on some pretext and was observed to meet in Clare Street a man-servant from one of the city clubs. The two then proceeded in the direction of Stephen's Green and the girl has not been seen since. The man was subsequently arrested on a charge of abduction and having been brought before a magistrate was remanded until Monday next, when the full facts in connection with the case will be elicited in the Police Court.

Glasgow Herald
January 24th, 1884

MYSTERIOUS CIRCUMSTANCE.

An elderly gentleman, named Thomas Southergill, of 4 Adelaide-road, suddenly disappeared from his residence yesterday and has not since been found.

Irish Times
October 5th, 1864

CRIME, MURDER AND EXECUTION

Few prisons are so proud to list their former inmates as Kilmainham Gaol, with its long line of political heroes and historical figures. Imprisoned alongside the named few were the unnamed many: criminals, desperate men and women, children, the guilty and the innocent. It was in a gaol and only in a gaol that the people who shaped Dublin — by leading it and by living in it — existed as near-equals.

A MORNING'S AMUSEMENT

A young gentleman named Montgomery Handsborough was brought up in custody before the magistrates, charged by a young man named Harry J. O'Brien, of Madras-place, Philsborough, with having stolen from him, about two months since, a gold pin worth a pound and five shillings. He stated that about two months since he met the prisoner at the Grand Canal Harbour, when they went to skate on the canal and, when at it for some time, the witness took off his coat, immediately upon which the prisoner put it on, and, after some time, took five shillings out of it and a gold pin, which he (the witness) wore.

Mr Porter asked when it was they went to skate?

Mr O'Brien said about three o'clock in the morning, about two months since, when the weather was very severe.

Mr Porter — At three o'clock of a winter's morning! And you took off your coat at that time, and in such a season?

Mr O'Brien — Yes, your worship; and when I thought to stop the prisoner, he ran off with my property.

Mr Porter — It's a most strange story that you should go to the Grand Canal at that hour and for such a purpose. Where did you spend the remaining portion of the night?

The complainant made no answer.

Mr Porter asked the defendant what he had to say in answer to the strange charge against him?

Mr Handsborough replied that the charge was a false one from beginning to end. He had never seen the complainant before nor was he in Dublin when the transaction alluded to occurred, but in Sligo, where he was doing business as a commercial traveller. He (the defendant) was never more surprised than when taken into custody that day on a charge of which he knew nothing. The witness, in continuation, said that he was the son of a clergyman and respectably connected, for the truth of which he appealed to Mr Fullam, then in the office.

Mr Fullam said that he knew Mr Handborough to be a most respectable young man and highly connected in the city of Dublin. Indeed he (Mr. F.) was never more surprised than when he accidentally saw him in the office in custody for a felony.

Mr Porter had no doubt of his respectability, but independently of that, it was quite clear the charge was a groundless one and he would therefore dismiss it.

Mr O'Brien said he would give his oath the defendant took his property.

Mr Porter observed that he might do so and be mistaken. To say the least of it, the charge appeared to him to be as novel as the act of going to skate on the Grand Canal at three o'clock of a morning during a winter of the utmost severity and, not content with that, taking off his coat to cool himself on the occasion.

The case was then dismissed.

Freeman's Journal
March 3rd, 1841

STRANGE SCENE IN DUBLIN CHAMBER OF COMMERCE ———— MEMBER CUT ON THE FACE ————

An incident of remarkable character took place yesterday afternoon in the Dublin Chamber of Commerce, says our correspondent. Amongst those in the reading room at 3 o'clock were Mr. Henry Joseph Farrell of York Street, a young man, and Mr. Robert Garratt, of Ballinasloe, both members of the Chamber. They had been standing at a window, when suddenly the others in the room saw the two men struggling. A number of men rushed over and took hold of Mr. Farrell, who, it is alleged, made repeated efforts to strike Mr. Garratt with a knife or razor. Mr. Garratt was cut about the face. The police were called in and Mr. Farrell was arrested, but, at the police station, neither knife nor razor was found on him. Mr. Garratt was afterwards treated for the wounds on his face. They are not of a serious character.

Glasgow Herald
February 19th, 1914

THREATENED AFFAIR OF HONOUR

At about half-past twelve o'clock on Sunday morning last, Mr. Duffey, one of the magistrates of the office was called up out of bed by a person who informed him that he apprehended a hostile meeting was about to take place between two gentlemen named Griffith and McDonnell, but he could not afford him (Mr. Duffey) the necessary information to enable him to arrest the belligerents. However, he directed that some of the police should be on the alert and act according as circumstances might require. The police accordingly exercised their usual vigilance and finally ascertained that an adjustment of the difference between the parties had been effected.

It was understood that a lady was the cause of the quarrel, which thus happily terminated without bloodshed.

Freeman's Journal
February 29th, 1832

IN FAVOUR

Pat Dunn presented as a loose and idle vagabond, who would not betake himself to labour or any honest means of industry, for a livelihood, traversed the presentment and the Jury found in his favour, as no person appeared to support the charge.

Freeman's Journal
February 14th, 1804

THE SCAM

It has become a practice with Agents of the bad-shilling-mongers to go about the town to buy different articles from shop-keepers and others and in order to enforce a currency of their truth; if any person refuses it, they threaten to give them a summons and many sooner than be so pestered accept the abominable payment.

Freeman's Journal
February 18th, 1804

THE MOUNTAIN ROBBER

Dwyer, who dubbed himself General, and his myrmidons, it is believed, will be sent to Botany Bay; he is much offended at being called a Mountain Robber and expresses much resentment against those who first bestowed upon him that elevated distinction.

Barth Tierney, who was to have been executed this day, according to his sentence, at the New Prison, for sheep stealing, has been respited for a week.

John McCabe was sentenced to have been executed this day at Kilmainham, for robbery, but as he was the person who discovered the horrid plot, formed in the gaol, to murder the Keeper and those under him in order to escape, it is hoped he will experience the clemency of Government.

Freeman's Journal
February 18th, 1804

A COLLECTION OF SECTARIAN MURDERS OF DECEMBER 1641 IN THE COUNTY OF DUBLIN.

About the 28th of December, 1641, the Wife of Joseph Smithson, Minister, was carried from Deansgrange, near to Stellorgan, from thence to Powerscourt and there she and her Servant hang'd.

• Henry Maudesley hang'd at Moore-town.

• Mr. Pardoe a Minister and William Rimmer a Packet-Post, murdered at Balrothery, Mr. Pardoe being afterwards cast on a Dunghill and his Head eaten with Swine.

• Derrick Hubert of Holm-Patrick, Esq. murdered the 2nd of December, 1641.

• Nicholas Kendiff murdered near Dublin, since the Cessation.

• Robert Fagan, murdered at Clunduff.

God's Goodness Visible in our Deliverance from Popery
Henry Maule
1733

THE DOLOCHER (A LEGEND OF THE BLACK DOG PRISON, DUBLIN)

**What old inhabitant of Dublin does not recollect the
BLACK DOG PRISON, which stood in Corn-Market?**

There happened to be a prisoner confined in this prison of the name of Olocher. He was under sentence of death for committing a crime, which, alas! not unfrequently stains even the criminal calendar – violation of female purity, accompanied by murder. The morning on which he was to undergo the last sentence of the law, he found means to commit suicide and thus escaped (if escape it can be called) the disgrace of being conveyed through the streets, exposed to the silent execrations of the multitude, on a cart to GALLOWS GREEN, now Baggot-street, then the common place of execution.

On the night after, the sentry, who stood at the top of a long flight of steps that led into Cook-street, was found lying speechless, with his gun by his side. When removed to the jail hospital, his senses and speech returned, but one side of his body appeared quite dead and powerless by a paralytic stroke, which he declared was caused by an apparition in the shape of a black pig. The next night, another sentry alarmed the guard and confirmed

the statement of the former. Consternation and terror spread on every side. The most sensible people of the day were of the opinion that Olocher had taken the shape of a black pig and had left the mark of his infernal vengeance on the first sentry and had carried off this last one, body and soul!

The next day a woman came before the magistrates, and made oath that she saw the DOLOCHER, (by which name it ever afterwards went) in Christ Church-lane – that it made a bite at her, held fast her cloak with its tusks, and that, through fright, she fled and left it with the monster.

At last, a set of brave, resolute fellows banded themselves together to rid the city of such a tormentor. They sallied out one night from a public house in Cook-street, at a late hour, armed with clubs, rusty swords, knives, and all such weapons as they could lay hands on, determined to slay every black pig they met. When any old pig would be difficult to kill, the women in the houses would shiver and exclaim, "Oh! they have him now – them are the boys – the devil's cure to the ugly beast" and such like tender expressions.

At this time Dublin was infested with such a multitude of pigs running about the streets that the bailiffs were obliged to go through the main streets and kill them with pikes and throw them into carts to carry them away. After such a night's slaughter, then, we might naturally expect that the streets were strewed over with dead bodies of pigs. No such thing. When morning came, not a pig, white or black, could be seen. How were they carried off? Infernal agency must have been at work in removing the carcasses. It was horrible.

However, no Dolocher appeared again that winter.

Dublin Penny Journal
November 24th, 1832

DUBLIN THREATENED

A letter was received by the police authorities at the Castle yesterday afternoon, purporting to have been forwarded by "Jack the Ripper," and stating that he intends visiting Dublin this week for the purpose of committing a murder. The letter, which was signed "Leather Apron" and "Jack the Ripper" is believed to have been written by some silly person who has been reading communications recently published in connection with the Whitechapel murders. The letter stated that a murder of a woman would be committed either in the east or west of Dublin; that the writer was determined to do away with unfortunates and his reason for doing so was because his sister had joined them. He defied Mr. Malton and all his detectives to discover him.

Freeman's Journal
October 10th, 1888

TWO DUBLIN-BORN SUSPECTS OF THE WHITECHAPEL MURDERS, BOTH DOCTORS.

Dr. Francis Tumblety (1835–1903) was a notorious quack who made his comfortable wealth from ineffective 'Indian Herb' medicines. He travelled the world with little care for the law or propriety. It is suggested that he stayed at a boarding house in Whitechapel around the time of the infamous murders. With a dubious medical honorific and supposedly exotic tastes, he made a natural Ripper suspect.

TUMBLETY'S PROTEGE TALKS
HE LIVED WITH THE DOCTOR AND WAS HIS CONSTANT COMPANION

"In the first place," said he, "the Doctor's name is Thomas F. Tumblety, and he is not an herb doctor any more than I am a street contractor. It was July 1882 that I applied for work at No. 7 University Place. I saw a big, fine-looking man standing on the stoop. He had on a braided English smoking jacket, black-striped trousers, Oxford ties, and a peaked cap. He told me there was no work for me in the house, but if I wanted to work he would give me a trial. I asked him what he wished me to do, and he said he was in need of a travelling companion. We walked upstairs to his room and he told me all about himself and I, afterwards, found it was true.

"He was born near Dublin, Ireland, in 1835, and was the son of a wealthy Irish gentleman. He was educated at the University of Dublin, where he graduated, as he showed by his diploma. He then studied medicine in Dublin and got another diploma, which he also showed me. In 1853, he left Ireland for America, landing in New York. Here he studied surgery and, when the war broke out, he was an army surgeon. He showed me his honourable discharge from the army and a number of personal letters from General Grant speaking of his efficiency and good conduct. About this time, his father died and left him a big lot of money. I don't know how much, but it kept him from having to do anything for a living."

New York World
December 5th, 1888

Dr. Thomas Barnardo (1845–1905) left Dublin in 1866 to study to become a doctor, with the aim of becoming a medical missionary. Although he has been suggested as a Ripper suspect by ripperologists Donald McCormick and Gary Rowlands, the basis of this accusation rests mainly on his work among the London destitute and his charitable visit to Elizabeth Stride shortly before her murder by the Ripper. The first of Dr. Barnardo's homes was opened in 1867 at 18 Stepney Causeway, London.

THE KILLING

Dr. Barnardo tells the following story of a visit on which he recently saw the woman Stride: "In the kitchen of No. 32, there were many persons, some of them being girls and women of the same unhappy class as that to which poor Elizabeth Stride belonged. The company soon recognised me and the conversation turned upon the previous murders. The female inmates of the kitchen seemed thoroughly frightened at the dangers to which they were presumably exposed. The pathetic part of my story is that my remarks were manifestly followed with deep interest by all the women. Not a single scoffing voice was raised in ridicule or opposition. One poor creature, who had evidently been drinking, exclaimed somewhat bitterly to the following effect: 'We're all up to no good and no one cares what becomes of us. Perhaps some of us will be killed next!' And then she added, 'If anybody had helped the likes of us long ago, we would never have come to this!' I have since visited the mortuary in which were lying the remains of the poor woman Stride and I, at once, recognised her as one of those who stood around me in the kitchen of the common lodging-house on the occasion of my visit."

East London Advertiser
October 13th, 1888

MYSTERIOUS MURDER
A FAMILY WIPED OUT
MANSION NEAR DUBLIN FOUND ABLAZE

A mysterious murder has been revealed by the burning of the country mansion known as La Mancha, close to Dublin. The mansion was owned and occupied by Joseph and Peter McDonnell and their two

sisters, a servant, and a gardener.

Early this morning, a workman observed the mansion ablaze. On the arrival of the fire brigade, the firemen found the gardener in a room in the basement with large wounds in the head. He was alive. Peter McDonnell was found naked in a bathroom, with his clothes spread over the dead body of Joseph McDonnell, who lay dead in another room. The upper part of the mansion, which was ablaze, contained practically the cindered bodies of the sisters and the servant.

The outer doors were barred. The fire had been started in different rooms on the ground floor and had spread to the upper floors. The McDonnells were reputed to be wealthy.

The police at first believed one of the brothers had lost his reason and, having set the premises on fire, had attacked the occupants.

The latest theory is that poison was the cause of death. Joseph McDonnell was the last number of the family seen alive. The others had not been seen since Monday, when McCabe the gardener saw Annie McDonnell in the garden, looking ill, and was told that Mary McGowan, the servant, was sick in bed. Joseph McDonnell later said Peter and Alice were also sick. McCabe says he went to a wake in Malahide and, when he returned, he found the mansion ablaze.

The *Age*
April 3rd, 1926

Henry McCabe (1877–1926) was, of course, lying about the wake. For fear of losing his job when the family sold the house, he had bludgeoned to death the six victims and set the evidence ablaze. He was hanged on December 9th, 1926, much to the relish of the press and public, and he appeared as a recurring character throughout Samuel Beckett's *More Pricks than Kicks*.

HUNG, BURNT AND SUNK

The method of executing Mrs. Herring this day, for the murder of her husband, was as follows: she was placed on a stool something more than two feet high and a chain being placed under her arms, the rope round her neck was made fast to two spikes, which being driven through a post against which she stood when her devotions were ended, the stool was taken from under her, and she was soon strangled. When she had hung about fifteen minutes, the rope was burnt, and she sunk till the chain supported her, forcing her hands up to a level with her face and, the flame being furious, she was soon consumed. The crowd was so immensely great that it was a long time before the faggots could be placed for the execution.

Gentleman's Magazine and Historical Chronicle
September 13th, 1773

THE POORLY EXECUTED EXECUTION

The two Murderers who were hung in Gibbets, at a little Distance from the New-wall, were put up in so scandalous a Manner that they fell down on Tuesday last and now lie on the Piles, a most shocking Spectacle.

Freeman's Journal
May 13th, 1766

PETER M'KINLIE, GEORGE GIDLEY, ANDREW ZEKERMAN, AND RICHARD ST. QUINTIN

EXECUTED FOR PIRACY AND MURDER, DECEMBER 19TH, 1765.

A plot was concerted between Peter M'Kinlie, the boatswain, a native of Ireland; George Gidley, the cook, born in the west of Yorkshire;

Richard St. Quintin, a native of the same country; and Andrew Zekerman, a Dutchman – for murdering all the other persons on board and seizing the treasure, which amounted to a hundred thousand pounds in dollars.

The conspirators were appointed to the night-watch on the 13th of November, when the ship had reached the British Channel; and, about midnight, the captain, going upon the quarter deck to see that all things were disposed in proper order, was seized by the boatswain, who held him while Gidley struck him with an iron bar and fractured his skull, after which they threw him into the sea. Two of the seamen, who were not concerned in the conspiracy, hearing the captain's groans, came upon deck, and were immediately murdered and thrown overboard.

Mrs. Glass and her daughter now came on deck and, falling on their knees, supplicated for mercy; but they found the villains utterly destitute of the tender feelings of humanity; and, Zekerman telling them to prepare for death, they embraced each other in a most affectionate manner and were then forced from each other's arms and thrown into the sea. Having put all the crew to death, the murderers steered towards the Irish coast.

Having thus massacred eight innocent persons, the villains proceeded to the mouth of the river Ross; but, thinking it would be dangerous to go up the river with so much riches, they buried two hundred and fifty bags of dollars in the sand. Having purchased each a pair of pistols and hired horses for themselves and two guides, they rode to Dublin and took up their residence at the Black Bull, in Thomas Street.

The wreck of the ship was driven on shore on the day of their leaving Ross; and the manner in which the villains had lived, their general behaviour, and other circumstances being understood as grounds for suspicion of their being pirates, an express was dispatched by two gentlemen to the Lords of the Regency at Dublin.

The prisoners being brought to trial, they confessed themselves guilty of the charges alleged in the indictment, and they were condemned and suffered death, December 19th, 1765, after which their bodies were hung in chains in the neighbourhood of Dublin.

The Newgate Calendar
December 19th, 1765

A PLACE FOR HERETICS

Hoggin-green, whereon St. Andrew's church now stands, which took up a large space of ground extending to the river Liffey, is often mentioned by the Irish historians, as the common place for the execution of criminals, among whom, to give one instance, Adam Duff O-Toole was in the year 1327 burned here for heresy and blasphemy. Part of this green is now called College-green.

The History and Antiquities of the City of Dublin: From the Earliest Accounts
Walter Harris Esq.
1766

John Atherton (1598–1640) was the Bishop of Waterford and Lismore, who was hanged, alongside his steward, John Childe, for sodomy.

On Saturday in the afternoon, being the 28 of November, and the next day after his Condemnation, I went to see him first, when having had some speech with him of the Scandall of the Fact, Justice of the Sentence, Misery of his Condition without Repentance, (of each of which he heard me long with silence) at length he asked me, if I were sent by any to him, when he understood I was not, but that I came of myselfe, he tooke me by the hand and replyed, I was very welcome to him, beleeved I had no other end but his good, that indeed he had been moved to send for me, but, being thus come of my selfe, he tooke me as sent of God. He acknowledged his stupidity and senslessnesse, desired me to preach the Law to him, to aggravate his sinnes by the highest circumstances, that he might grow but sensible of the flames of Hell: In subjects of this nature we spent neere two houres, when I left him plyable, onely with this assurance, that in Christ his sinnes were pardonable.

As a Preparative to the maine, I advised him to Lay aside all rich cloathing, and to put on the meannest he had. To let the Chamber be kept darke: To deprive himselfe of the solace of any company, but such as came to give him spirituall counsell and so to commit himselfe close prisoner to his owne thoughts, that if, upon necessity, any meat was brought unto him, he should eate it in a solitary way alone; And chiefly to give himselfe to fasting, even to the afflicting of his body, which he had so pampered, as a meanes to effect the sorrow of the Soule. To have his Coffin made and brought into his Chamber, which howsoever they were but small things in themselves, yet altogether were very conducible to a further end.

Nicolas Barnard, Dean of Ardagh
1642

THE PENITENT DEATH OF
A WOEFVLL SINNER;
Or The Penitent DEATH of
JOHN ATHERTON,
Late Bishop of Waterford in Ireland.

Who was Executed at DUBLIN
the 5. of December, 1640.
With some Annotations upon
severall passages in it.

As also the SERMON, with
some further Enlargements,
preached at his Buriall.

With a view to discredit both Bishop and Primate, a scandalous pamphlet was circulated after the execution, accusing Atherton of acts much less consensual. Attributed to the same Nicolas Barnard, it was titled "The Political Ballance, for 1754. The mock-patriot, for 1753. To which is added, the Case of John Atherton, Bishop of Waterford in Ireland, who was Convicted of Bestiality with a Cow and other Creatures, for which He was Hang'd at Dublin."

PRISONER HANGS HIMSELF IN A POLICE CELL.

Yesterday evening, quite a sensation was caused in the quiet little village of Ballybrack, County Dublin, in consequence of a desperate attempt of a man named John Kavanagh, aged 39 years, and a resident of the district, to hang himself in the strong room of the Royal Irish Constabulary Station. While he was confined, he was visited by Constable Maloney, who was horrified to find him hanging by the wall with a slight cord which had been passed round the window bar tightened in a loop on his neck. Constable Flynn, who arrived about the same time, instantly cut the prisoner down, and a messenger was despatched for Dr. Pim and Father Grimley, C.C. The constables applied artificial respiration and were assisted by Dr. Pim on his arrival, with the result that breathing was restored, but the prisoner remained and remains unconscious. Dr. Pim pronounced the case hopeless.

Belfast Evening Telegraph
August 16th, 1895

The

MELANCHOLY
INCIDENT
at
IRELAND'S
EYE

MELANCHOLY ACCIDENT-DEATH
OF A LADY BY DROWNING

CORONER'S INQUEST. Yesterday, Henry Davis, Esq., coroner for the north district of county Dublin held an inquest at Howth on the body of Mrs. Maria Kirwan, aged about 31 years, a remarkably fine-looking person, who had come to her death under the melancholy circumstances detailed in the subjoined evidence:

The first witness examined was Patrick Nangle. He stated that he was a fisherman living in Howth. The deceased directed him to come for her and her husband at eight in the evening; he did go at that hour, with his boat and the same three men; it was then very dark; Mr. Kirwan was by himself and, with one of the boatmen, named Michael Nangle, proceeded to look for Mrs. Kirwan and continued their search along the east side of the island, where at low watermark they found her lying on her back with her bathing-dress on her.

Michael Nangle examined – Mr. Kirwan covered the body with a sheet and a shawl and they conveyed it to the boat; they searched for the clothes, but could not find them, when Mr. Kirwan went higher up the rocks and discovered them; it was about ten o'clock when they found the body; Mr. Kirwan appeared to be in very great trouble when it was discovered.

Mr. James Alexander Hamilton, a medical student, stated that he had examined the body of the deceased; there were no marks of violence upon it; there were a few scratches, apparently caused by the rocks; the body presented all the appearance of that of a drowned person.

The jury found a verdict that the deceased had been accidentally drowned while bathing in the sea at Ireland's Eye on the 6th instant.

Freeman's Journal
September 8th, 1852

A HANDSOME MAN

Mr. Kirwan is a little above forty, a native of Mayo, but residing in Dublin for a considerable time. He is tall and well-looking; strongly built and the expression of his countenance corresponds with his strong limbs, broad chest, and duly-proportioned body. He is a painter by profession; and realised a handsome income from it, especially by drawing anatomical delineations, in which he excelled. His residence in Dublin was in a respectable quarter, No. II Upper Merrion-street, in a direct line between Merrion and Fitzwilliam-squares.

Mrs. Kirwan was about thirty; a native of County Clare, the daughter of an officer, Major Crowe. Her father is dead; her mother is still living and resides in Dublin. Mr. and Mrs. Kirwan had no children.

New York Times
January 15th, 1853

THE LATE CASE OF DROWNING
AT IRELAND'S EYE

It being understood that a public investigation into the circumstances connected with the death by drowning at Ireland's Eye of the late Mrs. Maria Kirwan, wife of Mr. William Kirwan, artist, would take place yesterday, at the Police-station, Howth, a reporter from the office was in attendance there at the appointed hour and was informed by Major Brownrigg, Deputy-Inspector-General of the Constabulary, that for the furtherance of the ends of justice and, in order to prevent ex porte statements which might be prejudicial to Mr. Kirwan from going to the public, it was thought advisable to exclude the press.

Our reporter then withdrew and we are, consequently, unable to publish any of the evidence.

We have been informed that the inquiry was conducted by Major Brownrigg – that eight or ten witnesses were examined and that the investigation was adjourned for eight days and Mr. Kirwan remanded for that period.

Freeman's Journal
October 9th, 1852

THE INVESTIGATION

There may be many cogent reasons shown for carrying on an investigation privately through even several adjournments, but we can admit none for the conclusion of a secret examination and the committal of a prisoner for trial without publication of the grounds on which he has been committed. Were such a course tolerated by the public or slurred over the press, it would lead us back to the dark ages of the Star Chamber, the black dungeon, and the torturer. It seems that the reason assigned for this unusual and most mischievous proceeding was that the publication of the evidence might lead to a public prejudgment of the case.

As to the case under consideration, the prisoner has been already prejudged from the mere fact of his arrest, so long after the admittedly unsatisfactory result of the coroner's inquest. There is not a single strange or unaccountable circumstance connected with the death of the poor young lady, the finding of her body, and the previous and subsequent conduct of her husband that has not been canvassed during the last week.

Freeman's Journal
October 16th, 1852

TO THE EDITOR OF THE FREEMAN
28, Stafford-street, 19th October, 1852.

Sir – In consequence of the evidence taken by Major Brownrigg, on the investigation relative to the above lamentable event, being private and, of course, not published, reports most injurious to Mr. Kirwan have been put into circulation and which, from the medical evidence given on the said investigation, as well as on the inquest, are completely negatived; I would, therefore (through your columns) request of the public to suspend their judgement on the matter until after his trial, which is to take place at the next Commission, on the 25th instant, when I have no doubt of his being fully and honourably acquitted.

I remain your obedient servant,

CHARLES FITZGERALD
Agent for Mr. Kirwan

They did not live happily together of late years; for another female, TERESA KENNY, was kept by him in the village of Sandymount, a mile from his residence, who went by the name of Mrs. KIRWAN and who bore him several children. She and they still live. To her, Mr. KIRWAN seems to have been much attached; as immediately on the interment of Mrs. KIRWAN, he had her and the children brought home to his residence.

New York Times
January 15th, 1853

ENIGMATIC CLAMOR

Rumours are in circulation, so universally that it would be ridiculous to pretend ignorance of their existence, about shrieks of distress and cries for mercy having been heard by fishermen who were proceeding home to Wicklow and that those cries appeared to come from Ireland's Eye about the time at which Mrs. Kirwan is supposed to have perished; yet who now can inform the public whether such rumours are founded on truth or are merely some of those wicked inventions that people afflicted with a morbid desire to circulate tales of wonder delight in fabricating?

Freeman's Journal
October 16th, 1852

"FOUND DROWNED"

An inquest was held and a verdict found according to appearances and the report of the boatmen: "Found drowned." She was interred at Prospect Cemetery, near Glasnevin, about a mile on the north side of Dublin. People talked and wondered; but the matter was beginning to pass away out of the public mind or to be replaced by other occurrences; when the public press announced that Mr. KIRWAN was apprehended and lodged in Kilmainham jail – the occurrence having taken place in the County – on a charge of murdering his wife.

Mr. WARBURTON, the Chief of the Detective Police, therefore set his men to work; the body was exhumed and, after two days investigation – upon the testimony of medical men that violence appeared to have been used, from the state of the body, especially of the lungs and from the position of the body when found and the circumstances connected with it, along with those other facts I have noticed before Mr. KIRWAN was committed for trial.

New York Times
January 15th, 1853

COMMISSON OF OYER AND TERMINER
The Hon. Justice Crampton and Hon. Baron Greene entered court yesterday at ten o'clock and took their seats on the bench.

THE QUEEN AGAINST WILLIAM BURKE KIRWAN

A true bill has been found against the prisoner, by the Grand Jury, at the previous October Commission, for the murder of his wife, Maria Louisa Kirwan, on the 6th of September, 1852; and on this indictment the prisoner was arraigned and having pleaded "Not guilty" on the application of the counsel for the Crown, the trial was postponed until the present Commission.

TRIAL OF WILLIAM BURKE KIRWAN FOR THE MURDER OF HIS WIFE.

Yesterday having been fixed for this trial, the Commission Court was crowded from an early hour. Long before the arrival of the judges the avenues leading to the court thronged with a vast number of gentry seeking admission. However, by the excellent arrangements made by the sheriff, abundant accommodation was secured for the bar and for the public press.

The galleries and seats in the body of the court were densely crowded with an assemblage, amongst which we observed a number of ladies.

Shortly after ten o'clock, the prisoner, William Burke Kirwan, was summoned to the dock by the clerk of the crown. Intense anxiety seemed to prevail amongst all present to catch a view of the prisoner, who shortly after issued, conducted by a deputy gaoler, from the door at the lower part of the dock, and ascended to the bar in front. The prisoner's demeanour was firm and collected. He is a respectable-looking man of about thirty-five years of age, stout in person, with dark hair and eyes. On being called on, he presented himself in front of the dock and leant on the bar. The indictment charged the prisoner, William Burke Kirwan, with having murdered his wife, Sarah Maria Louisa Kirwan, on the 6th of September last.

The prisoner was dressed with evident care and neatness. He wore a close-fitting paletot of blue black cloth, black satin stock, and black kid skin gloves. At the moment of appearing first in front of the dock to stand his trial for his life and subsequently during the address of counsel for the prosecution and throughout the progress of the evidence in sustainment thereof, the prisoner seemed to preserve a calm and collected demeanour. During the delivery of several portions of the evidence, the prisoner appeared to pay the deepest attention to the testimony of the witnesses and to observe the effect of their statements on the court and on the jury.

The prisoner having been formally arraigned and the offence with which he was charged having been stated to him:

The Clerk of the Crown (Addressing the prisoner) said, "Are you ready for your trial?"

Mr. Kirwan – Yes, I am.

Freeman's Journal
December 9th, 1852

TWO WITNESSES

Margret CAMPBELL, widow, who lives in Howth, proved that Mr. and Mrs. Kirwan lodged in her house in September last; they had but one room which they used as a sitting room and bed-room; observed quarrels between them; heard the prisoner call her a ____; heard him also say he would finish her; this was when they were about a month in the house; heard her say "let me alone;" next morning she was black after the usage she got.

Catherine M'GAR examined by Mr. Hayes. Lives at Howth; was engaged with the last witness in washing Mrs. Kirwan's body; there were wounds under and over each eye, as if torn, and a scratch on the temple; the mouth was swelled and the nose was crooked on the face; there was white slime on the mouth, blood was flowing from the inside of the left ear

The *Anglo-Celt*
December 16th, 1852

THE MEDICAL INVESTIGATION
James Alexander Hamilton – examined by Mr. Pennefather.

I am a medical student; I am studying for the profession and I have been attending lectures during the last six years; I have dissected during that time; I am familiar with the appearances presented by dead bodies; I was at Howth on the 6th of September last; I saw the body of the late Mrs. Kirwan on the following day at Mrs. Campbell's house.

I saw the face at first and I removed the cap and made a superficial examination of the head in order to see if there was any fracture or depression of the skull; I did not detect anything of the sort; there was a kind of mark or scratch on the right temple, such as would be caused by the rubbing of a body against a rock; it was only an abrasion of the skin; there were scratches or abrasions of the skin around the eyes; the eyes were shut; the eyelids presented a livid appearance, as if in a state of decomposition; I did not open the eyes. I remarked that the lower edge of one of the ears was cut, as if something had been biting at it.

Court Records
December 9th, 1852

CRAB BITE

Anne LACY Cross-examined by Mr. Curran. Has been forty years a nursetender; is certain from the appearance that the discharge she alluded to was not natural; has seen the bite of crabs.

To Mr. Smyly — There was nothing like the bite of a crab on the body.

The *Anglo-Celt*
December 16th, 1852

BODY UNEXAMINED
James Alexander Hamilton – examined by Mr. Pennefather.

I did not examine the body very closely; I did not examine the private parts; I did not see any blood where she was lying; I did not raise up the body in order to examine it.

Court Records
December 9th, 1852

MEDICAL TESTIMONY

We do not feel ourselves called upon to enter into an examination of all the evidence adduced at the inquest held on the body of the late Mrs. KIRWAN or at the trial of the accused party, but we would refer especially to the medical testimony brought forward on the part of the prosecution; and anything more unsatisfactory or inconclusive we have never read.

The *Lancet*
December 25th, 1852

AFTER DEATH

GEORGE HATCHELL – EXAMINED BY MR. SMYLY.

I am a physician and a surgeon; on the 6th of October last, I was called on to make a post-mortem examination of the body of Maria Kirwan; that was thirty-one days after death.

Court Records
December 9th, 1852

IN DEFENCE OF MURDER

Dr. Hatchell concluded his examination in chief thus: "From the appearance of the body, I am of opinion that the death was caused by a sudden stoppage of respiration. I think, from all the appearances of the body, pressure must have caused the stoppage. I am of opinion pressure was the sole cause." What pressure? Where applied? If upon the chest or upon the mouth, how, we ask, does the Doctor account for the existence of the froth at the mouth at the time when the body was found? On cross-examination the doctor stated that "engorgement of the lungs was not compatible with drowning alone"! Any statement of a more unfortunate character could not have been given at a trial where the life of a fellow-creature was concerned. It is perfectly well-known to the profession that engorgement of the lungs is a common condition of those organs in the bodies of drowned persons. Probably it is the most common of all the post-mortem appearances found in the bodies of persons who have died from suffocation by drowning. Where, then, is the evidence which proves that the unfortunate lady died from the effects of pressure? Proof of pressure upon the chest there is none. Proof of pressure on the mouth there is none.

Looking, therefore, at the medical evidence, as called in support of the prosecution, it is our decided opinion — and that opinion is not recorded until after the bodies of hundreds of suffocated persons have been seen by us — that, in not a single particular, does the medical evidence sustain the dreadful accusation which has been made against the wretched man who is now under sentence of death.

The *Lancet*
December 25th, 1852

CONVICTION OF THE PRISONER

Eleven o'clock, p.m.

According to the arrangement, Mr. Justice Crampton returned to court at 11 o'clock to ascertain whether the jury had agreed. Even at that late hour, the building and the approaches to it were crowded with persons anxious to learn the result of the trial.

His Lordship having taken his seat, the jury were called out and the prisoner was placed at the bar.

One of the jurors wished to hear the evidence of Dr. Adams again.

Mr. Justice Crampton said that his note-book was at home, but, if there was any portion of the evidence he desired to hear, he might be able to give him information upon it.

A Juror asked if his lordship could state to them the evidence of Doctor Adams as to what the appearances on the body might be caused by – whether by accidental or forcible drowning?

Mr. Justice Crampton said the evidence of the doctor was that congestion of the lungs and the other parts might arise from simple, innocent drowning or by drowning caused by forcible immersion.

The jury then conferred together for a short time.

The Clerk of the Crown asked – Gentlemen, have you agreed to your verdict?
Foreman – Yes.

Clerk of the Crown – How say you, gentlemen, is the prisoner, William Kirwan, guilty or not? You say he is GUILTY.

Freeman's Journal
December 10th, 1852

THE VERDICT

Mr. Justice Crampton – William Burke Kirwan, it becomes now my very painful duty to pronounce upon you the sentence necessarily consequent on the crime of which you have been convicted. That crime is murder – a crime denounced both by human and Divine law as the most heinous crime that man can commit against his fellow-man. Now William Burke Kirwan, according to the evidence and the finding of the jury, yours is not an ordinary murder – great as the guilt of murder always must be. You raised not your hand in daring vengeance against a man from whom you had received or thought you had received injust provocation or insult, but you raised your hand against a female – helpless, unprotected female – one whom by the law of God and man, was entitled to your protection even at the hazard of your life and to your affectionate guardianship. That victim was the wife of your own bosom. In the solitude of that rocky island to which you brought her on that fatal 6th of September, under the veil of approaching night, where there was no hand to stay and no human eye to see your guilt, you perpetrated this terrible – this unnatural crime. And what was your motive? It appears that, for years, you had been leading an immoral profligate life. You were living with a female who was not your wife, by whom you had a large family and, thus circumstanced, it would appear, you married the unhappy lady whose death you no doubt now deeply regret.

I cannot hold out to you one ray of hope of pardon on this side of the grave. The die is cast and I fear it is against you and cannot be reversed. Consolations you can have none now.

Having said so much, it now remains for me to pronounce upon you the awful, solemn words of the sentence fixed by the law. [Here his lordship assumed the black cap, which caused a shudder to pass through the crowded court] That sentence is that you, William Burke Kirwan, be taken from the place where you now stand to the place from which you came, the jail, and that from thence you be taken to the place of execution, the gallows, and that you be there hanged by the neck until you be dead and that your body be buried within the precincts of the prison to which you are now confined. And may the Lord have mercy upon your soul.

Court Records
December 10th, 1852

DENIAL

Mr. Kirwan, who appeared to be affected by the concluding words of the learned Judge, then leaned forward over the front of the dock and said, My Lord — Convinced, as I am, that all my hopes in this world are at an end, I do most solemnly declare, in the presence of this court and that God before whom I shortly expect to stand, that I had neither hand, act, or part, or knowledge of the death of my late wife, Maria Kirwan; and I may further state, that I never treated her unkindly in my life, as her own mother can testify.

The prisoner then retired from the dock. The 18th of January is fixed for the execution.

The *Anglo-Celt*
December 16th, 1852

——————— **A RARE EXECUTION** ———————

It is more than a dozen years since we have had an execution in Dublin; and the crime, in this case, is not of the ordinary Irish type. We have, unhappily, but too much blood-shedding in Ireland, but it is usually the effect of passion heated by intoxication or the murder is that of those whom Ribbonism teaches to slay landlords, agents, or bailiffs. Such murders as this one occur more frequently in England and the habits in which they originate are more frequent: sporting with female chastity, the unrestrained gratification of lust, and the reckless disregard of the domestic obligations.

But a better use to make of such awful and deplorable occurrences than for national recrimination is for parents of all classes to impart to the young a religious education, founded on the culture of the moral principle and the enforcement of holy obligations, as the only effective safeguard against the temptations to such fearful crimes and for all who have escaped them the thankfulness and a desire to keep others free.

Mr. KIRWAN, since his conviction, continues to receive the visits of clergymen; is calm and in health; but solemnly asserts his innocence. There is not, however, any public sympathy nor any likelihood of a movement for procuring his pardon.

New York Times
January 15th, 1853

In the wake of his conviction, a large number of pamphlets was published investigating Kirwan's possible innocence, including:

The Kirwan Case: illustrating the danger of conviction on circumstantial evidence, and the necessity of granting new trials in criminal cases, published by J.B. Gilpin, Dublin, 1853.

Defence of W.B. Kirwan, to which is appended the opinion of Alfred. S. Taylor, M.D., F.R.S., that "No Murder was Committed," John K. Boswell, 1853.

Is Kirwan Proved Guilty? Anonymous, 1853.

Exposure of an Attempt to impute the Murder of Messrs. Crowe and Bowyer to W.B. Kirwan, J.K. Boswell, 1853.

On the Medical Evidence of Death from Drowning, in Relation to the Case of W.B. Kirwan, Alfred S. Taylor, M.D., 1853.

On the True Height of the Tide at Ireland's Eye on the Evening of the 6th September, 1852, the Day of the Murder of Mrs. Kirwan, Samuel Haughton, 1857.

DEFENCE OF WILLIAM BOURKE KIRWAN, CONDEMNED FOR THE ALLEGED MURDER OF HIS WIFE, AND NOW A CONVICT IN SPIKE-ISLAND

When Mr. Boswell was requested to investigate the circumstances in connexion with this mysterious case, he found the public mind prejudiced by the malicious and false reports, industriously circulated, that Kirwan had murdered several other persons and, amongst others, his brother-in-law Crowe and a Mr. Bowyer, which latter charge led to a long investigation before the Commissioners of the Metropolitan Police, during which investigation the convict was removed to Spike Island.

In considering the circumstances of this singular case, it becomes absolutely necessary to trace the sources from which these reports sprang and, on looking into the information taken by the Crown, it appears that on the 21st September, 1852, one Maria Byrne, a person who for years has been proved to have systematically persecuted Kirwan, made an affidavit, in which, among other statements, she swears –"That having ascertained that the said Mr. and Mrs. Kirwan had left the residence No. 11, Upper Merrion-street, about three weeks ago, she, suspecting that Kirwan had taken his wife to some strange place to destroy her, made inquiry as to where the parties had gone and that she had no doubt on her mind that the said Mrs. Kirwan was wilfully drowned by her husband (the convict) and that she had strong reasons to believe he (Kirwan) made away with other members of his family under very suspicious circumstances." To this person is to be attributed the first suspicion that Mrs. Kirwan was murdered by the convict and that it was she who also spread reports that Kirwan had murdered Crowe and Bowyer and charged him with the murder of her husband.

The next person who charged the convict with murder and robbery is a Mrs. Bowyer. This person has claimed, from the Commissioners of the Dublin Metropolitan Police, a large quantity of pictures, which are now in Kirwan's house and which, she alleged, were, in the year 1837, stolen from her husband, many of them being of great value. On an investigation and examination, it appears that almost all the valuable paintings so claimed by Mrs. Bowyer are paintings which were sent by third parties to be cleaned and an immense number were copies made within a few years by Kirwan himself. She also claimed a modern book-case full of books, which Mrs. Bowyer told the police-constable was just as it was, with all the books in it, when stolen from her husband in 1837. The books, on examination, were found to be nearly all of a modern date, having been published between 1845 and 1852. Yet, upon the testimony of such witnesses, was the charge of murder got up against the wretched and absent convict. Mrs. Bowyer some years since was in a lunatic asylum.

Alfred S. Taylor
1853

He was convicted at Dublin in December 1852, for drowning his wife on the little island of Ireland's Eye, off Howth Harbour. Reprieved on the eve of the execution, he served thirty years and more in the prison at Spike Island and was released an old and broken man. On the evidence, it seems to us most emphatically a case of "Not proven" and inquiries after the trial severely discounted the evidence of the most material witnesses for the prosecution. But Kirwan's irregular life and conjugal infidelities had raised a strong prejudice against him: he was convicted not for murder, but for adultery.

The *Spectator*
June 27th, 1908

In fact, Kirwan saw out only 26 years of his life sentence. He was released in March 1879, under the condition that he leave Ireland and never return.

NEW THEATRE ROYAL, ABBEY STREET

FOR SIX NIGHTS ONLY

THE GREATEST WONDER OF THE AGE,

MONSIEUR CHYLINKSI!

(late Lieutenant in the Rifle Brigade of Augustow, in Poland), who will make his first appearance on *MONDAY & TUESDAY, March 8th & 9th,* in the Chemico-Physical and Gymnastic Representations, in Four Characters, viz.,

**THE ATHLETIC MAN! THE MODERN HERCULES!!
THE FIRE KING, AND THE POLISH SALAMANDER!!!**

In the First Character of the ATHLETIC MAN, Monsieur Chylinski will exhibit a variety of feats of Physical Force and prove that they may be gained by continual and persevering exercise, united to a knowledge of the Mechanical Structure of the Human Frame.

In the Second Character, as the MODERN HERCULES, he will give several extraordinary examples of his great Strength and Gymnastical Exercises.

In the Third Character of the FIRE KING, he will go through a variety of Chemical Experiments.

In the Fourth Character of the POLISH SALAMANDER, he will give a variety of astonishing proofs of his Incombustibility by a selection of Experiments.

ON THIS EVENING,

Wednesday 24th instant, and following days, Mr. G. will repeat his new Piece, entitled

THE ENCHANTED HOUSEHOLD;
Or, The Randoms of a Ventriloquist.

Which includes Fourteen Characters, all acted and transformed by Mr. Gallaher alone.

FOR HIGH-CLASS WORK AT MODERATE PRICE TRY

PATRICK CAHILL
OPTICIAN TO THE POPE

13 WELLINGTON QUAY, DUBLIN

All articles of merit have been imitated and so has this popular luxury, of which the public will pray beware.

ROYAL SPORT OF COCK-FIGHTING

ON MONDAY, the 25th of FEBRUARY, the first of the Septenial Mains between the Gentlemen of the KING'S COUNTY and the Gentlemen of the COUNTY of FERMANAGH, for TWENTY GUINEAS a Battle, and FIVE HUNDRED the Main or Odd Battle, begin fighting at the New Pit, Farmers' Repository, Stephen's-green.

The Noblemen and Gentlemen Members of the Sod and Jockey Club, intend dining at Falkener's Tavern, Dawson-street, each Day, and for that Week the Club will be open to all Gentlemen Sportsmen that wish to join in the amusement, provided that they are introduced by a Member.

The Gentlemen who intend to Dine will please so leave their name at the Bar.

SUPERFLUOUS
HAIRS PERMANENTLY REMOVED

without mark or scar by Electrolysis; *consultations free; hours 10 to 5. – Miss Read,* 5 DAWSON-STREET, DUBLIN.

SOCIETY FOR PSYCHICA[L]
A LECT[URE]
Will be Deliv[ered]
THE ANTIQUARI[AN]
(6 STEPHEN'S [GREEN])
By
MR. W. B. Y[EATS]
On
GHOSTS AND D[EMONS]
FRIDAY, 31ST O[CTOBER]
CHAIR TO BE TAKEN [BY]
SIR WM. BARRE[TT]
Admission - Members, Free; N[...]

THIS DAY PUBLISHED, Price **2s. 6d.**,

ANALYTIC RESEARCHES IN SPIRIT MAGNETISM, considered as the Key to the Mysteries of Nature and Revelation, and the Medium of Communication with the Invisible Worlds; all tending to indicate the Importance of **ECSTACY** and **CLAIRVOYANCE,** *and the Psychological Phenomena of*

ELECTRO-BIOLOGY

By Hill H. Hardy, A.M., T.C.D.,
BARRISTER-AT-LAW
Author of *"Geometrical Properties of Polygons."*
Dublin: GEORGE MASON, 24, D'Oiler-street.

Lady with business of Land or her own view early marriage; young widow not objected; strictest secrecy.

MONSTER SALOON,
CRAMPTON COURT, DAME-STREET,
CROWDED NIGHTLY WITH THE ELITE OF SOCIETY.

ENGAGEMENT EXTRAORDINARY OF
MR. AND MRS. HARRISON IN
THE TERRIFIC COMBATS
WITH THEIR WONDERFUL
NEWFOUNDLAND DOGS!

ENTHUSIASTIC RECEPTION OF
YANKEE SMITH;

LOUD APPLAUSE OF
MISS BEAUCHAMP,
the celebrated Serio-Comic Singer;

DECIDED HIT OF
MR. BISHOP,
the eminent Scottish Vocalist, who will appear in his splendid Native Costume;

IMMENSE APPROBATION OF
MISS ANNIE EARLE,
the Sentimental Vocalist;

GREAT EXCITEMENT CREATED BY
THE BROTHERS CARR
in their pleasing entertainment

FINE WINES, BRANDIES, &C., KIDNEYS AND OYSTERS.

LEONARD'S A[...]
37 HENRY STREET,
AND 36 TALBOT STREET, DUBLIN;
Ordinary Blaud's Pills 6 ½ per gross.